LIVING IN THE
NUMBER ONE COUNTRY

LIVING IN THE
NUMBER ONE COUNTRY

REFLECTIONS FROM

A CRITIC OF

AMERICAN EMPIRE

HERBERT I. SCHILLER

SEVEN STORIES PRESS

New York / London / Sydney / Toronto

Chapter One incorporates previously published material from "Striving for Communication Dominance: A Half-Century Review" by Herbert I. Schiller, published in Daya Kishan Thussu, ed., *Electronic Empires—Global Media and Local Resistance* (London: Arnold and New York: Oxford University Press, 1998). Reprinted by permission of the publisher.

Chapter Three incorporates previously published material from "Digitized Capitalism: What Has Changed?" by Herbert I. Schiller, published in Howard Tumber, ed., *Media Power, Professionals and Policies* (London: Routledge, 2000), 116-120. Reprinted by permission of the publisher.

Chapter Four incorporates previously published material from "The Social Context of Research and Theory" by Herbert I. Schiller, published in Ingunn Hagen, ed., *Consuming Audiences? Production & Reception in Media Research* (Creskill: Hampton Press, 1999). Reprinted by permission of the publisher.

Chapter Six incorporates previously published material from "Living in the Number 1 Society" by Herbert I. Schiller, published in *Gazette: The International Journal of Education* 60, no. 2 (April 1998). Reprinted by permission of Sage Publications.

SEVEN STORIES PRESS, 140 Watts Street. New York, NY 10013, www.sevenstories.com

In Canada: Hushion House, 36 Northline Road, Toronto, Ontario M4B 3E2

In the U.K.: Turnaround Publisher Services Ltd., Unit 3, Olympia Trading Estate, Coburg Road, Wood Green, London N22 6TZ

In Australia: Tower Books, 9/19 Rodborough Road, Frenchs Forest NSW 2086

Library of Congress Cataloging-in-Publication Data

Schiller, Herbert I., 1919–2000
Living in the number one country: reflections from a critic of American empire/ Herbert I. Schiller—A Seven Stories Press 1st ed.
    p. cm.
    ISBN 1-58322-028-3
    1. Communication—Political aspects—United States. 2. Communication—Economic aspects—United States. 3. United States—Politics and government—20th century. I. Title.

P95.82.U6 S343 2000
302.2'0973—dc21

00-020284

9 8 7 6 5 4 3 2 1

College professors may order examination copies of Seven Stories Press titles for a free six-month trial period. To order, visit www.sevenstories.com/textbook, or fax on school letterhead to (212) 226-1411.

Book design by Cindy LaBreacht

Printed in the U.S.A.

FOR LUCY AND ETHAN

ACKNOWLEDGMENTS

This book could not have been published without the total dedication and commitment of my partner and wife, Anita Schiller. There were other major contributors. Here I list only Dan and Zach Schiller.

I would like to acknowledge the continuing support of Sandy Dijkstra, and the efforts on my behalf of Paul Abruzzo, Joyce Evans, and Jenny Troutner.

H.I.S.
La Jolla, California
October 1999

CONTENTS

INTRODUCTION
ONE LIFE, ONE CENTURY

For more than sixty years my life's experiences have been shaped by the large-scale events of the twentieth century. From depression childhood to insecure student, from governmental employee to enlisted soldier, from military government worker to university professor, this introduction is a résumé of some of the encounters and episodes of a turbulent era as they impinged on one life.

I grew up in New York City in the depression years, having been born in 1919, two years after the Bolshevik Revolution and one year after the end of the bloody World War I. In my small family, hard times began in 1929. In the fall of that year, at the onset of the Great Depression, my father, a craftsman jeweler, lost his job. Except for local relief work, he remained unemployed until the war in Europe broke out. In 1940 he was hired by an aircraft factory, brought back into production by war-stimulated orders.

In the 1930s we escaped destitution and dispossession. We remained in our one-bedroom apartment—my parents slept on the living room couch and gave me the bedroom. Nourishing food was never absent. Occasionally clothing was purchased, mostly for me. My uncle helped pay the monthly rent. My mother found cleaning jobs in the public school system. She came home exhausted from her day's work and the long subway ride and prepared the evening meal.

Yet these economic difficulties did not interrupt my education, and I attended public school, high school, and the free City College of New York (CCNY), from which I graduated in 1940. Though I did not contribute to the family income, I did work and make enough to pay for transportation, lunch, and small entertainment expenditures, a few movies, subway rides, occasional sodas. All of this is to say that, compared with millions of others, our existence was far from desperate, though never free of anxiety.

There was always the money worry and the uncertainty of the near future. There were frequent quarrels, most of which had an economic origin. It was at this time that I could see how my father's continuing joblessness was viewed by my mother as weakness and inadequacy. In my separate life—I was out of the apartment most of the day—I knew this was unfair and wrong. Yet there seemed no way to contradict it. This atmosphere penetrated my being with sadness and resentment. I have never forgotten how the deprivation of work erodes human beings, those not working and those related to them. And from that time on, I loathed an economic system that could put a huge part of its workforce on the streets with no compunction.

As I see it now, there was one condition favorable to my

general well-being and development that I could not appreciate at the time: the total absence of formal religious observance in our household. It was not the consequence of deliberate choice or a grounded atheistic ideal. It was, rather, the complete preoccupation of my parents with getting food on the table and securing for their son the best education they could not actually afford.

Not only was everything else secondary, it did not even come into question. In this somewhat austere secular environment, I may have missed some rich cultural history. But I have always felt fortunate to have escaped from the confines of orthodoxy and parochialism. I was starting out with one less pair of shackles. I am aware that today, this notion of liberation has been rejected by many in the postwar years.

It should not be concluded that this freedom from religious ritual and orthodoxy made for an enlightened adolescence. In my high school freshman class, for example, a straw poll was taken about student preferences in the approaching 1932 national elections. I was one of a handful of kids that chose Herbert Hoover. The overwhelming majority supported Franklin Delano Roosevelt.

My choice was influenced entirely by what I heard my parents say. No other political views at that time entered my consciousness. That an unemployed worker and his wife would, in the depth of the Great Depression, vote for the candidate of big business says much about early-twentieth-century mind control.

When my father finally got full-time, well-paying work in a war factory, I learned another enduring lesson. Ten years of human wastage through unemployment finally was overcome by a still vaster and more impersonal human wastage, the oncoming of world war. This was the not-so-secret stimulus to production and employment in the privately organized U.S. economy. Without it, there was no telling when the economic crisis would have ended. I, too, benefited from the newly created war economy. After worrying through four years of college about finding work when I would graduate, the problem dissolved in an explosion of war-connected employment.

After Pearl Harbor, the war became a total national involvement, which pulled me in the following year. But from 1941 until my induction, the expanding war agencies in Washington were hiring, and, like my father, I got a war-created job. Washington offered an escape from my family-monitored and financially restricted New York life. For a year, the freedom of a relatively well paid job; my own, though shared, apartment; new friends; and the inescapable feeling of living on borrowed time until military service, generated great energy.

I joined a union, the United Federal Workers. I tried to recruit, mostly unsuccessfully, other employees. This attracted the attention of the dollar-a-year industrial executives who staffed the upper echelons of my agency, the War Production Board, who had not left their antiunion sentiments and practices back at their home companies.

Washington, D.C., in 1941–42 was a still segregated metropolitan area. The dynamic center of the war effort to defeat the Nazis and the fascists was itself a profoundly antidemocratic place. To a twenty-one-year-old raised in New York City, Washington's overt racism was a shock.

Education and daily routines in New York at the time were scarcely less segregated. Getting to City College, which was located at 138th Street and Convent Avenue, daily on the trolley, I passed through an adjacent sector of Harlem, the major black community. City College itself, in my recollection, did not have one black student in my 1,000-strong class. Perhaps there were a few African-Americans on the campus, but I never met or saw them. So New York apartheid was very real, but not understandable, at least to me then, as a legally coercive system.

Washington was different. The evidence of apartness, buttressed with force, was everywhere. I remember my sense of disbelief on crossing the bridge from the District of Columbia into Virginia and seeing signs that warned that "Negroes" were not permitted in local parks. In government cafeterias in Washington, separate dining rooms and food lines rigidly divided the races. Washington offered a stark prelude to what I would soon encounter overseas in the former colonies of the imperialist European states.

Drafted in the fall of 1942, I spent a year in a dozen army camps up and down California, mostly in southern California around Los Angeles, and in and out of the desert. In that year before being shipped overseas, I marveled at how the war was experienced in this loony part of the country. It was a big party that even I, an anonymous corporal, could wander into from one weekend to the next. Stepping out onto the highway to hitch a ride to Los Angeles could lead to a two-day merry-go-round of invitations to house parties throughout the area.

The war plants in southern California were working three shifts. Thousands of workers would come off their jobs at midnight, revved up and raring to join the nightlife that was organized on a round-the-clock schedule—restaurants, bars, bowling alleys, movies, dance halls, whatever. Consumption needed no encouragement, coming after a ten-year depression. It was supported by full paychecks.

These scenes contrasted wildly with my arrival in North Africa in September 1943, and my limited travels in Europe over the next two years. It was shockingly clear that, with few exceptions, Americans had no idea of the costs of the war. The impoverished countrysides, the bombed cities and villages, the haggard civilians, the acute shortages of the most elemental necessities, escaped the U.S. troops' notice. In the United States (not all but many) people were, if not partying, then leading satisfying lives, while the world was suffering unimaginable disasters.

In American army camps, the post exchanges—commissaries—stocked huge quantities of goods. Overseas life for noncombat soldiers—a relatively small percentage of the Armed Forces—was not a hardship existence. In many places, post exchange goods were blackmarketed by the GIs, contributing further to the enormous gulf separating the U.S. war experience from that of much of the world's population. Over the decades that followed, this gap in common experience partly explains the recklessness of U.S. leadership in many international encounters, and the widely differing attitudes to the risk of provoking a new war that separated American from world public opinion.

Almost two and a half years of my military service was spent in North Africa: Tunisia briefly, Algiers for six months, and Casablanca in Morocco for two years.

Before my overseas sojourn, my knowledge of mass poverty was pretty vague. I knew of bread lines in Depression-stricken America. I had seen slums in New York City. I heard about "Hoovervilles," shack towns on the outskirts of cities during the bad years of the 1930s. Yet none of these prepared me for what I found in North Africa.

In Casablanca, *bidonvilles*, tin can settlements, made up of discarded oil drums and cardboard cartons, surrounded the city, homes to thousands of people. These unfortunates shared one or two open water faucets and utterly lacked the most primitive sanitation facilities. Though the French were still the reigning colonial power across the rim of North Africa, it was clear, even in 1943, their rule was coming to a close. The French still made air raids on defenseless villages viewed as troublesome. Local newspapers were routinely censored, often leaving blank columns on the pages. These efforts were in vain, however.

The U.S. presence was the new pole of power. American heavy transport filled the roads. Large numbers of local people were employed at the many U.S. installations. At night, on the edge of a GI audience watching an outdoor screening of an American film, Moroccan kids and adults followed the images intently. The new power, with its material riches and dazzling images, was nonchalantly elbowing out the once dominating authority. This pattern was to be repeated in one colonial site after another. Inevitable as it turned out to be, it also carried with it the expectation of improvement, material and social. What would the United States do with its enormous capability to influence developments worldwide? Despite initial widespread hope, as time passed, the United States became a modernized model of domination.

For me, the North African interlude was a powerful prod to consciousness. What later came to be called, always euphemistically and often deceitfully, the Third World, the developing world, and, most recently, "emerging markets," continues to be, as I then began to understand it, the part of the world where great numbers of people live and die under frightfully deprived conditions. In their midst are enclaves of lavish wealth and power. Over time, I realized that these tragic destinies continue to be ordered by foreign owners and investors, and local oligarchs, whose one public concern is undisturbed profit making. This was the burden that the "advanced" West, and the United States in particular, imposed, and continues to impose, on the poorest and weakest peoples worldwide for half a century.

My next significant learning experience came after the defeat of Nazi Germany and its subsequent occupation by victorious British, French, Soviet, and U.S. forces. I returned from North Africa demobilized in the late fall of 1945 and spent three months at home in New York City. I did not seem able to jump into the postwar boom that was swirling about me, and so I traveled to another damaged society: I accepted a civilian job with the U.S. Military Government in Germany. By March 1946, I was living in Berlin, and part of the presumably democratizing process in West Germany.

In Germany I received hard-to-come-by instruction on how a terribly battered industrialized, market economy is rehabilitated by a self-interested class ally. This was not everyday learning. Well before I went into the army in 1942, I had a good stretch of higher education. I graduated from college with a degree in social science and a major in economics. I also had a master's degree in economics from Columbia University.

I mention this only because one might have assumed that this much formal education would have produced an individual knowledgable about the basic relationships that comprise the prevailing system of production and consumption. Wrong assumption! My university education had been a shallow and superficial enterprise. The central driving forces of the economy I lived in were either ignored or left vague, to the point of meaninglessness.

When I returned to the States in mid-1948, thoroughly disgusted with official U.S. policy in Germany, it was evident that a terribly wrong and falsified assessment of Russian aims had gained wide and growing acceptance. Anticommunism, which dated back at least to the Russian Revolution thirty years earlier, had grown to constitute a full-blown national environment.

But there was still some resistance to the anticommunist propaganda steamroller that had the enthusiastic support of the national information dispensers. Elections were coming in November, and in July, the Progressive Party, with former Vice President Henry Wallace and Senator Glen Taylor heading the ticket, was founded. It seemed to be successfully questioning the anti-Soviet foreign policy of the Truman Administration. I attended their founding convention rally in Shibe Park, Philadelphia, days after returning from Europe, and felt buoyed by the enthusiasm and spirit that infused the huge gathering.

Soon enough I received another lesson in applied political science. To meet the challenge of the Progressives, the Truman forces quickly adopted, in collaboration with the Republicans, two tactics. First, a frenzied hunt for Communist spies in the government, real or imagined, fueled the rising anticommunist sentiment in the country.

At the same time, Truman demagogically sent an emissary and offered to meet with the Russians. This was the proffer of good faith and moderation to balance the hysteria the basic policy was provoking. These initiatives served to persuade the electorate that Truman was pursuing a reasonable course and that the Progressive alternative, of active cooperation with the Soviets, could be safely ignored. Truman squeaked by, and the Progressive Party disintegrated.

This was the onset of an era of implacable anticommunism, what came to be known as McCarthyism, though it far outlasted the Senator. It continued as a low-grade infection in the 1960s and 1970s and flared up aggressively in the Reagan 1980s. It is by no means extinguished in the 1990s.

Facing this atmosphere, saturated with fear and hatred for a good part of my life, has required constant examination of my own beliefs and of my ability to analyze the social scene. How could I be so distant from the general thinking of the population? Was it a personality matter, some strained sense of uniqueness? Not too much time was spent worrying about this, but it did remain a source of wonderment.

Later, my attention became focused on how the process of inculcation worked. Who organized it? How were the messages shaped and transmitted? Who controlled the dissemination networks? How far did the networks extend? But before being able to study these matters, by the early 1950s I had a family with two children, and I was the only wage earner. I taught full-time at the Pratt Institute in Brooklyn, an arts school, and part-time, at night, at the City College business school at Twenty-third Street and Lexington Avenue.

These were trying years. My beginning salary at Pratt was less than $2,000, the teaching load a punishing five-course schedule, with two additional courses at night at City College. Some days I would have seven classroom preparations. Most of the time I was exhausted. The pervasive political atmosphere was overhung by the reality of investigating commissions, firings, the blacklist, and the generalized repression and coercion. Most of this was marginal to my own life but I knew many for whom these developments were traumatic. Notwithstanding some popular nostalgic sentiments about that period in the 1990s, I couldn't wait to see the end of the political environment of the 1950s, and the miasma in which that decade was engulfed.

After Truman's election in November 1948, oppositional views to the course that Washington was pursuing were less and less visible, eventually approaching underground status. The world was being reshaped by American power, though anticommunism provided the daily news and entertainment menu. A curtain had come down in America, smothering free discussion.

And so it was in 1949–50, when most middle-class professionals were scurrying as rapidly as they could away from anything that they feared might bring them to the attention of the new vigilantism, that I chose to become a part-time, unpaid, radical journalist. Starting out in an era of semi-hysteria, I began to write weekly or biweekly articles on American foreign economic policy for the Labor Research Association (LRA), a tiny research group that critically scrutinized the corporate features of the American economy. The director of LRA at the time was Bob Dunn, one of the most considerate and sweetest men I've ever met, then or since. Working with Dunn was the remarkable Grace Hutchins, who had spent a lifetime in the radical movement.

My connection to LRA was limited to delivering personally, whenever I had written it, a short article I hoped might challenge at least a small sector of the approved and distorted conventional press coverage that overwhelmed the nation. I did not use my own name; the byline was LRA. Willing as I was to contribute my analytical skills, such as they were, to express an alternative view, I had no desire to be subjected to the kind of ferocious state-directed intimidation that was all too evident and pervasive.

I couldn't help feeling more than a little anxiety. Each visit I made to the LRA office on East Eighteenth Street in New York City to deliver my fragment of oppositional journalism seemed fraught. Paranoia prevailed in the country at large, and I was entitled to exhibit mine by walking rapidly, or averting my face, and worrying incessantly that I was being photographed entering the building or the office. This continued for several years, though my productivity, and my paranoia tailed off after the mid-1950s.

My full-time job at the Pratt Institute began in 1950, and my starting salary, as I said, was around $2,000. It increased incrementally about a thousand dollars a year. The other job, teaching evenings at City College, was on an hourly basis, something like $4 an hour. Pitiful as these jobs were monetarily, they would have disappeared immediately if my extracurricular activity had become known.

What were the subjects I addressed in this forbidding time? One overall theme ran through my work. It continues to this day. It was, and remains, the use of American power—so dominant over the period—to extract privilege and prevent social change that might limit that privilege. The places and instances where this was occurring spanned the globe, but I gave my attention to those locales about which I had some, though limited, personal experience. One was the Western European social order, which was "threatened" not, as was asserted by our leadership, by Soviet aggression, but by its own indigenous radical movements.

At the end of World War II, largely as a result of their antifascist leadership during the war, the major parties and movements in Europe were led by Communists and socialists. In both France and Italy the Communist parties were the biggest political formations. In the early fall of 1945, on a trip to France while still in the army, I remember the very visible presence of the French Communist Party—the billboards, placards, announcement of rallies, and the like—in Nice, hardly the industrial belt of the country.

The U.S. government, with the active assistance of the CIA, did everything it could to weaken and disrupt these movements. The records of these interventions remain secret, fifty years later, despite continued presidential assurances that the documentation will be released.[1]

Even so, we know plenty. Noam Chomsky, condensing a good bit of the history of the process in postwar Europe, wrote:

> Marshall Plan aid was strictly contingent on exclusion of Communists—including major elements of the antifascist resistance and labor—from the government; "democracy," in the usual sense....
>
> In France, the postwar destitution was exploited to undermine the French labor movement, along with direct violence. Desperately needed food supplies were withheld to coerce obedience, and gangsters were organized to provide goon squads and strike-breakers, a matter that is described with some pride in semi-official

U.S. labor histories, which praise the AFL for its achievements in helping to save Europe by splitting and weakening the labor movement (thus frustrating alleged Soviet designs) and safeguarding the flow of arms to Indochina for the French war of reconquest, another prime goal of the U.S. labor bureaucracy. The CIA reconstituted the Mafia for these purposes, in one of its early operations. The quid pro quo was restoration of the heroin trade. The U.S. government connection to the drug boom continues until today.[2]

The other focus of my writing was the former colonial territories, many of them recently politically liberated but actually totally dependent economically, militarily, and culturally. The not-so-secret U.S. objective was to secure this vast area with its huge populations and untold resource wealth, for private corporate exploitation. As was the situation in Western Europe, the populations and most of the leadership in the ex-colonial world had a different vision, a socially planned perspective, generally with its own specific characteristics.

This, of course, created big problems for U.S. policy makers. But even in this early postcolonial period, U.S. power was applied relentlessly to recovering the region(s) for profit making. All of this proceeded under a terminology that manipulatively linked freedom and choice with private ownership while associating noncapitalist regimes of varying character with tyranny and despotism and, worst of all, communism.

Having seen the devastation in Europe and the unspeakable

conditions in colonial North Africa, I found it astonishing that
the efforts being made in many places to find new ways to
approach social reconstruction were regarded by Washington as
threats to peace and American well-being. It was this astonish-
ment, and frustration at the refusal of the informational system to
divulge what was occurring, that drove my journalistic impulses.

One of my first pieces, in August 1949, examined American business and governmental perspectives that sought to
reverse the very mild postwar reforms of the British Labour
Party. This was significant, I thought, because it demonstrated
early on the willingness of U.S. capitalism to intervene outside
the country against working people on behalf of capital. More
important, it was an early display of American leadership's
unwillingness to accept the most limited modifications in an
ally's private profit-making economy that might ease the lives
of England's majority.

At that time, and ever since, U.S. power, governmental and
private, has come down on the side of capital against the living
standards and well-being of the laboring classes. Unemployment and austerity have been the policies endorsed and
applied to troubled economies by U.S. checkbook-holding
leaders. These interventions constitute the history of the last
half-century and are as much a part of the concluding years of
the twentieth century as they were fifty years ago.

In 1998 U.S. Treasury Secretary Robert Rubin, on an inspec-
tion tour of the world market system the United States largely

dominates, had this advice to offer the newly elected South African government, which was faced with the cumulative devastation of centuries of colonial rule. Before it took power in 1994, the African National Congress, it may be remembered, had a socialist outlook and favored nationalization and full employment. Rubin brushes this aside. His formula for the South Africans, hardly updated from the recommendations his predecessors gave to the British in 1949, emphasizes "austere budgets, open markets, vigorous competition and the sale of state-owned companies... and greater flexibility from labor unions."[3]

Unfortunately, this advice can be disregarded only at a terrible price. If the South Africans demur, their access to capital will be shut off and their currency and economy put under siege. Here, as in all the other instances of U.S. pressure and intervention around the world, social alternatives are foreclosed and nations and people locked into the dominant system, with all its inequalities and ferocious imbalances.

Efforts to improve working conditions and allow labor a stronger voice in decision making, wherever undertaken over the decades, have been bitterly, and generally successfully, resisted by Washington power. The disappearance of the non-market sector of the world—the disintegration of the Soviet Union—has further strengthened the worldwide offensive of property against labor.

A second vital interest of the new U.S. superpower in 1945 was, and continues to be, the economic overlordship of as much of the world as possible. This became my other journal-istic sphere of attention. In achieving this end, the great eco-nomic wealth and power of the United States has been used as a lever either to bribe or to coerce the compliance of others. The weaker the targeted country, the stronger the exactions demanded. Consider, for example, the conditions extracted for Western "aid" from South Koreans, and other Southeast Asian states, in 1997–98.

The *New York Times* account is headlined "Asia's Surrender: Reeling from Blows to Their Economies, Countries Agree to Financial Concessions" (December 14, 1997). Elaborating, another report described the mechanism of control:

> On a general level, the [IMF's] growing role in overhauling the private sector is making it a more explicit advocate of the style of capitalism long championed by the United States, cen-tered on free markets, reduced government involvement in business decisions, and more openness.... The fund has also become the closest thing the world has to a global financial regulator.[4]

The world has changed greatly over the last fifty years, but the technique of extorting advantage, through the use of heavily conditioned economic assistance, from weak or ailing economies has been a durable feature of the period. Actually, one of the earliest applications was while World War II was in its concluding stage. The instrumentality was the United Nations Relief and Rehabilitation Administration (UNRRA).

Established as an emergency relief organization to alleviate the hunger and distress that would accompany the liberation of the Nazi-occupied areas of eastern and central Europe, UNRRA provided an early model for later international bodies that would engage in the aid business. Its membership was international—as far as that was possible at that time—but its chief contributor, and therefore most influential member, was the United States.

The efforts of the United States to steer UNRRA away from helping Eastern Europe and the Soviet states, unless they complied with rules set down by the dominant grant-giving state, were a preview of what would become the standard pattern when the war was over and the United States took up its self-assumed role as the world's rule maker.[5]

One international organization after another came into existence at war's end. The United Nations, with a number of related, function-based organizations (World Health [WHO]; Food and Agriculture [FAO]; and Educational, Scientific, and Cultural [UNESCO]), formed the overarching structure. But of greater influence were the economic structures, also newly created, that operated outside the UN framework. These followed the organizational pattern of the UN, with one crucial difference. The national contributions to these economic-financial bodies were calculated on a rough scale of economic strength, as they were in the UN; but while in the UN each state had one vote, voting rights in these structures were distributed according to the member's economic contribution.

It followed that in the World Bank and in the International Monetary Fund (IMF), the two most important institutions, the United States had, by virtue of the size of its contribution, the dominant voice and the absolute prerogative to veto any decision that displeased it. This "principle" has disfigured international decision making since 1945 and has been the source of an untold number of grievous decisions and actions. Yet viewed from the perspective of the North American power complex, it has been of inestimable value in securing as much of the globe as possible for the U.S.–led market system.

I looked into the World Bank's structure and activities in a piece I wrote in 1950, titled "The World Bank: Agency for Wall Street's Cold War," which provides an account of how economic assistance was withheld from poor, socialist, or socialist-inclined states in the postwar years. Fifty years later, in dramatic contrast, capital is being lavishly funneled into many of those places—Russia, Indonesia, Mexico, Korea, and so on—as long as they adopt the private market economy and abandon their public sector. Then and now, withholding or disbursing capital is the United States' lever of control.

By the late 1950s my career as a radical journalist had taken a new direction. This was due in part to a gradual slackening of the national repressive atmosphere, though U.S. global interventions continued unabated. It also coincided with an opportunity to join the faculty of the University of Illinois in 1961.

This afforded me space to research and write on a regular basis—a very welcome change from my heavy teaching schedules in New York, which had taken almost all my energy.

Though communication was a relatively new subject in academic studies, it became the core of my work for twenty-five years. Personal, local, and global factors combined to encourage my new area of interest. The University of Illinois had a strong record in the field from early on, housing several of the first communication scholars. Dallas Smythe, for example, who had singlehandedly created the study of the political economy of communication, was still teaching there, and we became friends. When Dallas left the University to return to Canada, I inherited, so to speak, his graduate course. Additionally, the Bureau of Economics and Business Research, to which I was appointed, was led by an experienced and wonderfully open-minded director, V. Lewis Bassie. Bassie, without any questions asked, permitted me to do my research—a considerable extension of the bureau's customary projects.

Actually, Bassie's work was in economic forecasting. He was one of the few at that time who still remembered and understood the susceptibility of a market economy to damaging booms and busts. He predicted a downturn that didn't materialize, as the long postwar boom temporarily interrupted the business cycle. This put him outside the conventional thinking and had the effect of making him an exemplary overseer of my own against-the-mainstream work.

But larger forces were at work. U.S. interventions around the world were multiplying: Cuba, the Dominican Republic,

and Vietnam, where U.S. troops were fighting a barbarous
colonial war with the most advanced weaponry. How these
bloody and cruel events were being presented to the American
public offered a key to understanding how the far-reaching
control of popular consciousness in the country was being
managed. The war also offered a unique example of how the
control system could be challenged, with the rapid growth of a
real opposition.

The antiwar movement grew stronger as the war continued, but the propaganda for the war was no less intense, as the
specter of one anticommunist domino after another falling to
the Reds became an unrelieved Washington refrain. And the
media were fully complicit in supporting the war in the early
years of the conflict. What turned the tide was the strength of
the Vietnamese resistance, as the costs of waging the war
reduced the national budget to a shambles. The decisive cost at
home, however, was in the lost blood and lives of American
youth. When domestic anger and shock reached a level dangerous to social stability, parts of the establishment and the
media broke the prowar consensus and the unraveling was
underway.

Even in such a relatively remote place as central Illinois,
long the site of a "jock" university with row upon row of frater-
nity and sorority houses, the war jolted the campus out of its
play routines. Student demonstrations led twice to university
administrators summoning the National Guard. Mirroring the
temporary loss of conventional governing control, some of the

players on the football team showed up at antiwar parties and events. This was one of those all-too-infrequent times in the last half century when the experiences of (enough) people propelled them to reject the policies and explanations of the governing class. As also could be expected, after the event, the media claimed that they had prompted the antiwar effort with their reporting. Washington and the military knew better. The staggering losses of American youth changed the informational climate, and eventually government policy.

Vietnam is now more than a quarter of a century behind us, and the changes in the domestic informational system since the war have been far-reaching. What was at that time a powerful and concentrated structure has become a globally integrated multimedia machine, owned by a few dozen, at most, giant private communication enterprises. Yet before this pyramid of global information power became the new standard, I was engaged in the short-lived efforts of the ex-colonial world to restructure the global economy into a more equitable and life-enhancing living space. For a few brief years, numbers of poor nations, some still led by their liberation heroes—Nehru in India, Sukarno in Indonesia, Tito in Yugoslavia, Castro in Cuba, Nasser in Egypt, Ben Bella in Algeria, Nkrumah in Ghana, and others in Kenya, Angola, Mozambique, and elsewhere—sought to change economic and informational structures worldwide.

Here again, as in Europe, in 1945–50, an opportunity appeared to move away from the disastrous policies of domination and privilege. Once more, on a global grid, the United

States and a few allies resisted substantive changes that would have reconfigured the global distribution of resources.

In the end, the Third World's demands came to nothing. With the exception of the oil-producing states' attempt to gain greater control of their vital natural resource, the ambitious objectives of the ninety-plus poor countries possessed no leverage to apply to the Western dominators, especially the United States. There were no indispensable resources they could withhold. Their military capability was practically nonexistent. They were compelled, for lack of alternatives, to issue their challenge in the international bodies created after World War II; essentially the United Nations and its subsidiary organization, UNESCO (the United Nations Educational, Scientific, and Cultural Organization).

The have-nots' claims to a new international economic order, and subsequently a new international information order, were expressed in the meetings of these bodies. Invariably, after a comprehensive exposition of the inequities and injustices of the prevailing structures, the issues would be voted on, and recommendations for changes would be passed by overwhelming majorities. And that was the end of it; there was no mechanism for implementation. More to the point, the powerful nations in control of the system had no intention of accepting even the most modest limitations on their privileged arrangements. The demands put forth to improve these crucial areas of human existence, however valid and just their bases, had no chance of overturning the realities of economic, military, and technological power. Actually, the situation corresponded closely to my previous historical experiences in Germany. All the same, I spent a good deal of my time in the late 1960s and throughout the 1970s involved in the global informational debate.

Mass Communications and American Empire (1969) and *Communication and Cultural Domination* (1976) were my contributions to the global discussion.[6] Attacks on these works evidenced the semihysterical opposition in the West to any structural modifications of the privileged corporate networks of information control. For example, the executive director of Freedom House overstated my importance to the opposition in grotesque and even comical terms, casting me in the role of ventriloquist to a distinguished Chilean diplomat, Juan Somavia, at that time director of the Latin American Institute for Transnational Studies (ILET), and currently the Chilean ambassador to the United Nations.

Analyzing a speech given by Somavia at that time, Freedom House found that "at the outset, Somavia describes, exactly as Schiller does, the origins of the Third World media challenge: the continuation of colonial domination from the 'center' to the 'periphery,' from the transnational power structure to the dominated Third World; from the controller of information to its recipient." It concluded: "Woven into [Somavia's conclusions] were Herbert Schiller's concepts": for instance, the use of "center" to refer to dominating countries and "periphery" for the dominated nations.[7] Much as I might want to, I cannot take credit for these terms, which were first formulated by distinguished Latin

American dependency theorists, one of whom is, at this writing, the president of Brazil.

Yet still larger social forces were at work, and well before the "Third World Media Challenge" to the West subsided, new transformations were making the have-nots' goals of economic and informational equality recede further. These developments coincided with changes in my personal living and working arrangements.

In the fall of 1970 I left Illinois and moved to southern California, where I became a professor of communication in a newly created college at the University of California, San Diego. Once again, my education received an unexpected and unconventional widening. The new college had been established as a result of student demonstrations—in fact, by the seizure of buildings. The aim of the students was to secure an educational enterprise that would seriously concern itself with the needs of the nation's "minorities," African-Americans, Chicanos (Mexican-Americans), and native Americans.

That the demands of the students were partly met, temporarily, was itself remarkable. But it reflected the turbulence of the times and the volatile condition on the nation's campuses during the Vietnam War. In this instance, the students, and some faculty sympathetic to their goals, were authorized to organize a curriculum for the new college. Four main areas were chosen for study: Third World studies; science and technology; urban and rural studies; and communication. Each was to focus on the special needs of the minority students. This domestic objective was of a piece with the Third World movement for a new international economic and information order, with local specifications.

I was hired, after intense student interviews—a rarity in itself—to head the communication program. Departmental status was promised quickly. The importance of this is hard to exaggerate; a program has no autonomy and cannot make its own appointments. These are the prerogatives of a department.

I set forth as the "coordinator" of the program, with three nontenured faculty borrowed from the literature and sociology departments—hardly a secure base for a project seeking to develop major changes in the educational enterprise. My obligation to the new college and the students, as I understood it, was to create a meaningful set of courses in the communication field that would enable those enrolled to develop their understanding and consciousness and overcome the mental servitude instilled in oppressed classes and groups.

I interpreted my task as trying to explain how the powerful communication system in all its spheres (film, television, publishing, the press, recording, and education) was structured, and how it created, or at least justified, inequality. This perspective, as might be expected, did not secure the confidence and administrative support that was accorded conventional modes of study. Our tiny unit was treated by administrative power as an annoying infection that it hoped to quickly cauterize.

One circumstance alone protected and enabled us to survive in the initial period: The students found our relatively few courses stimulating and meaningful. The daily news—what it reported, how it reported it, and what was left out or distorted

—supplied my major texts. Much of this material appeared in *The Mind Managers* in 1973. (Years later, in 1981, I used television to disseminate similar critiques in a series of half-hour shows titled *Herb Schiller Reads* The New York Times.[8]

Our popularity with the students continued to grow. Our enrollment numbers exceeded those of most of the traditional departments. This guaranteed our survival, since the university has become no less a retailer in need of "customers" than any department store, yet general campus support for our efforts continued to be meager. Across the university, communication was regarded as a subject lacking substance and taught by ideologues. Compounding the problem, no established discipline would admit to the slightest possibility that its field might have an ideological slant.

The suspicion of communication on the campus was reinforced by extra-university pressure. One example was an article by two nationally syndicated columnists, Roland Evans and Robert Novak, describing me as a white radical brought in to mold the minds of minority students. These minds were regarded by the writers, and probably by many others, as malleable clay, waiting to be shaped by manipulative fingers.

Our courses critically examined the actual world; and another development worked steadily on behalf of our program. Silently, and almost invisibly, the underlying structure of the national economy was changing. These transformations included the growth of the service sector and the relative decline of the industrial sector, the ever-enlarging role of the transnational corporation in production and distribution, and the rapid development of new communication technologies, the propellants of an increasingly information-using economy.

In the mid-1970s these developments were still in formation, but their presence could not be ignored. Their implications and impact on the national scene soon became overwhelming, and we were affected locally as well. Communication and "information society" became daily popular references. How then could the university disregard a sphere of knowledge that was becoming ever more prominent in the popular mind and press? It couldn't, and we owed our survival in part to the emergence of an alleged information society.

While the structural shifts noted above were making themselves felt throughout the economy, equally significant changes were underway in the national information condition. It was to these that my attention turned in the 1980s and '90s. Let me give the context.

My wife, Anita Schiller, had been a librarian since the 1950s. When we moved to Illinois, she joined the University of Illinois Library Research Center, the first such unit in the country devoted to library research issues. Her assignment was to select and study questions of concern to libraries. One of her first efforts was to design and carry out a survey of college and university librarians. Her main finding, at the time revelatory, was that though women comprised the largest part of the library workforce, they were the "disadvantaged majority" in terms of salary and job level.

Beyond this study, which received national attention, the Library Research Center offered a unique opportunity to gain an overview of what was happening in the library field. And this was no parochial landscape. Libraries were caught up, almost unwittingly, in the most fundamental changes occurring in American society. The momentous shifts in the information world, were first turning up as library problems affecting the daily work and experiences of the nation's leading libraries and librarians.

For example, computerization, privatization, and commoditization of information first appeared as library developments. As such, their implications for the economy at large were practically disregarded. Libraries historically had been treated as marginal institutions—respected and given rhetorical support, but far outside the areas of decision-making power. It was not surprising, therefore, that fundamental trends appearing first in the library sphere, passed almost unnoticed in the general perception of what were considered important national developments. My own recognition and partial understanding of what was occurring I attribute completely to Anita's experiences, commentary, and early writings on these trends. A first indication of what was happening with remarkable speed was the privatization of information as commercial online database services were introduced, and libraries that historically had been centers of information freely available to all users found themselves engaged in policy making about whether charges should be levied on the new computer services—the fee versus free debate.

This was and is no trivial issue. It goes to the heart of a profound change spreading across the economy—the steady expansion of commercial transactions at the expense of public and community activity. And it was only one of many issues that emerged in the library field but were connected to the transformation of the whole economy by spreading computerization under corporate auspices. The libraries served also as early experiment and testing centers for familiarizing the workforce and general population with the new instrumentation. In the process libraries, starting with the big research facilities, became early users and enthusiasts of the new information technologies. This contributed greatly to the success of the changes underway.

As these developments became more clear, it was also apparent that the entire social order was being reshaped in a most undemocratic way, while the beneficiaries publicized these changes as freedom-enhancing developments. Much as the "democratization" of Germany was heralded, as was "development" in the Third World, the shaping of a corporate global electronic environment has most recently been presented as promising universal benefit.

These contradictory conditions set the central themes of my writing and work in the 1980s and '90s. My task, as I interpreted it, was to analyse and explore the contradictions and deceptions of the proponents of the new information age. I tried to demonstrate how the industrial and technological transformations then sweeping across the country benefited the already most powerful force in the system—the big global corporations. Additionally, I claimed that despite all the changes observable in daily life, the main characteristics and dynamics of the centuries-old private profit-making system remained in place, if not intact.

In 1998 the International Monetary Fund (IMF) largely replaced the World Bank as the source of capital to beleaguered states. Its structure of decision making is basically the same as that of the World Bank. The determining criteria for obtaining capital from the IMF are no different, though perhaps more onerous, than they were fifty years ago. There is today, hard as it is to imagine, even less balance in the world community than there was in 1945. Investor and creditor interests are paramount; social need and an equitable society hardly come into consideration. When President Clinton visited Moscow in September 1998, he told the bankrupt Russians that U.S. aid would be resumed only if the international investors were satisfied with the terms. The Russian people, on the edge of total impoverishment, didn't come into the discussion.[9]

In the early postwar years, two other closely related goals motivated Washington's international policies. The central objective was to secure as large a part as possible of the ex-colonial world for the world market system. The dangers of slippage at that time seemed very high. Nationalist leaders with social vision were in the command positions of many new nations; how to forestall such developments occupied the attention of U.S. military and intelligence services and the financial establishment.

Yet while doing everything it could to thwart alternative courses of social development in these new states, American power also sought to reassure their leaderships, and the U.S. public, that its intentions were honorable and that, unlike the old imperialists, the United States sought no special advantages.

In the half century since the end of the war, U.S. companies have been transformed into global enterprises, extending their interests from raw materials acquisition to production plants and financial subsidiaries in scores of countries. In 1949 the British and the French and others were told that they had to restrict their consumption and discourage their workers from demanding decent wages because of the competition of the powerful, postwar American economy. In 1999 countries are given the same advice, with the justification that the competitive pressure of the "global economy" demands it.

Basically, the issue is who benefits in a privately structured society. Capital is in a position to see that its interests are taken care of, but it doesn't quite come out that way as public information. How could it when the worldwide presence and activity of U.S. corporate business are now handled by massive public relations firms, phalanxes of lobbyists, and information massaging services that make the earlier "Point Four" claims sound primitive?

Shuttling back and forth over a half century's developments can be confusing. Yet these historical observations of a time long past serve to highlight the extraordinary feature of the entire age—the pervasive application of one power's authority to the world scene. Washington's policies and actions today are the direct descendants of those prevailing over a span of five decades. Modifications in some cases have been made, and new practices introduced, but the fundamentals are unchanged. The United States remains the center of a globally expansive system, one that still strives to eliminate critical opposition. The system administrators, governmental and business, have had to take into account global power shifts— the disappearance of the rival Soviet sphere, the emergence of China as a potentially great world force, and the efforts of Europe to become a unified entity and a likely economic challenger to the United States. Withal, the impulse of Washington and the power complex it represents remains one of command and domination.

Many of the deformations in American society of the twentieth century have their roots in a vast enterprise of deception that has reached into almost every crevice of the social order. A mixture of concocted threats of aggression, external and internal, has been central to a masterfully arranged scenario whose creation and staging have been effected by thorough collaboration of the leaders of the country's main institutions. Little of this social transformation has been planned or coordinated; it developed out of the drives and assumptions of a newly emerged corporate order that found itself in an unprecedented position of global power.

Military force, espionage, and disinformation campaigns

figured into and contributed to the U.S. effort to keep as much of the world as possible in its bailiwick. The record over the period is one of incessant military interventions, military buildups, spy scares, witch hunts, classifications of information, universities sanitized by academic purges or the threat of them, and Cold War curricula. Paraded before us in popular culture, on TV and in films, has been an army of invaders and secret operatives who perform, in full special-effects regalia, dramas that numb the intellect and channel the passions. The total absorption in commmercial translations that permeates the tightest echelons of the social order filters down to all levels.

What then can be concluded from this bare-bones review of more than half a century's social developments seen from the point of view of their personal impact on one individual? Perhaps it has been the need to express my concern, often my outrage, over a course of events that could have had different outcomes. I could not imagine either accommodation or passivity in the face of what sometimes seemed lunatic, at other times calculated, aggressions against ordinary people's lives and well-being. In 1998, for example, a government report estimated that the United States had spent over *five trillion dollars* since World War II on nuclear weaponry.[10] We would be living in a different world had those staggering expenditures been invested in a socially productive manner.

Yet far more costly has been the unwillingness of U.S. leadership to allow other nations and peoples the freedom to pursue different directions in their economic and social life. American policy and actions have for half a century repeatedly frustrated initiatives for a better and more diverse world. It is an awesome indictment.

NOTES

1. Tim Weiner, "CIA, Breaking Promises, Puts off Release of Cold War Files," *The New York Times,* July 15, 1998, A-13.

2. Noam Chomsky, *Deterring Democracy* (New York: Verso, 1991), 343.

3. Donald G. McNeil, Jr., "Visiting South Africa, Rubin Sides with the Free-Marketers," *The New York Times,* July 15, 1998, C-5.

4. Richard W. Stevenson and Jeff Gerth, "IMF's New Book: A Far Deeper Role in Lands in Crisis," *The New York Times,* December 8, 1997, 1.

5. Herbert I. Schiller, "The U.S. and UNRRA," Ph.D. diss., New York University, 1960.

6. Herbert I. Schiller, *Mass Communications and American Empire* (New York: A. Kelley, 1969); Schiller, *Communication and Cultural Domination* (White Plains, N.Y.: International Arts and Sciences Press, 1976).

7. Leonard R. Sussman, "Mass News Media and the Third World Challenge," *The Washington Papers,* Vol. 5 (46) (Beverly Hills, Calif.: Sage, 1977).

8. Herbert I. Schiller, *The Mind Managers* (Boston: Beacon Press, 1973); *Herb Schiller Reads* The New York Times, Paper Tiger Television, 1981.

9. "Clinton and Yeltsin Press Conference," *The New York Times,* September 3, 1998, A-10.

10. *Atomic Audit* (Washington, D.C.: Brookings Press, 1998), quoted in Peter Passell, *The New York Times,* July 9, 1998, C-2.

CHAPTER ONE

NUMBER ONE AND THE POLITICAL ECONOMY OF COMMUNICATION

T oday the United States exercises mastery over the global communication/cultural sphere. How did it happen? One conclusion is inarguable. America's political leadership has, since the first days of its new order, been fully aware of the key role communication would play in its superpower pageant. Reviewing the last half-century of tumultuous change in the communication/cultural arena, a few sweeping generalizations seem warrantable.

The first is that the U.S. (capitalist) state, contrary to many reports, is alive and, if not well, at least still in charge. This conclusion does not apply necessarily to other states in the global economy, but in the United States very significant functions are still performed by the state. Certainly in the sphere of communication it is no paper tiger. To the contrary, representing the core interests of capital, the state has demonstrated unusual vision. It has acted frequently, with initiative and decisiveness, to assure the promotion of the ever-expanding communication sector to its present status as a central pillar of the economy.

A second general feature of this period is the effort, marked by many variants, to persuade the public that a new era has arrived—one that breaks the connection to earlier times. The argument generally dismisses many existing structural or institutional relations—like the adversarial relation betweeen labor and capital—as obsolete. The game, it is said, is a new one, with no roots in the past. History, by this criterion, is useless for understanding the present. This especially destructive ideological notion undermines any understanding of the social process and how to change it.

A third conclusion, reached after five decades of witnessing continuous changes in the structure, content, and dissemination of the cultural/communication industries and their growing concentration, is the legitimacy and essentiality of political economy—the blend of economic and political interests—as a means of grasping ongoing developments. The ever-popular proposition that the cultural/media sector can be regarded as autonomous and free-standing has been belied by material conditions that have generated a configuration of cultural production that simply cannot be explained without recourse to political economy.

Let us examine these propositions in more detail.

THE STATE AND THE PROMOTION OF U.S. COMMUNICATION MASTERY

In the late 1990s there has been a strong insistence in governing and academic circles that the market is the solution to all problems, that private enterprise is the preferred means to achieve solid economic results, and that government is, as one economic analyst recently put it, "the enemy."[1]

The last half-century's record, however, is of government initiative, support, and promotion of information and communication policies. It is important to understand that this has been deliberate policy, taken by every administration from World War II up to and including the Clinton White House. Capital, and its administrators, have consistently denied the legitimacy of government intervention on behalf of social needs, while being most solicitous for expenditures that facilitate the coercive and moneymaking sectors.

The principle—vital to the worldwide export of American cultural product—of the "free flow of information" has made a universal virtue of the cultural industries' marketing requirements. John Foster Dulles, possibly the most aggressive secretary of state in the postwar years, regarded "the free flow" as the single most important issue in foreign policy.[2] Even before the end of World War II, the Pentagon made military aircraft available to U.S. publishers and senior editors to circle the globe and hector leaders in eleven allied and neutral countries on the virtues of a free press—defined as a privately owned one—and the free exchange of information.[3]

The goverment did everything in its considerable power in the early postwar years to establish the free flow doctrine as a universally accepted objective. Assistant Secretary of State William Benton, for example, in 1946 put it this way: "The

State Department plans to do everything within its power along political or diplomatic lines to help break down the artificial barriers to the expansion of private American news agencies, magazines, motion pictures, and other media of communication throughout the world.... Freedom of the press—and freedom of exchange of information generally—is an integral part of our foreign policy."[4]

In Congress, in international fora such as the UN and UNESCO, and at international conferences, U.S. representatives pressed relentlessly for the free flow. To be sure, there was another benefit from this advocacy. Beside the material advantages it offered to U.S. companies, it facilitated an ongoing propaganda windfall at the expense of the nonmarket sector of the world (USSR and the like) which was organized on a completely different basis. Free flow, as articulated by U.S. officials, invariably emphasized the unacceptability of the doctrine to state-managed societies and easily made it appear that virtue was being rejected for evil.

State support for the cultural industries, however, was not limited to ideological initiatives. A wide-ranging program of U.S. material assistance to many countries came into operation after the war. The Marshall Plan (1948–1951), for example, was a model for all the foreign "aid" programs that succeeded it. One of the many features of the plan was tying dollar grants to a recipient's acquiescence to opening its market to U.S. cultural exports, film in particular.[5]

Stipulations of this nature have remained a feature of U.S. foreign aid in its many forms; they have become the basis of

U.S. world trade policy, and have been incorporated in World Trade Organization Agreements.

Canada, the foremost example of a country exposed to an almost unrestricted U.S. flow of information, occasionally attempts to safeguard at least a niche for its own cultural activity. But the World Trade Organization, heavily influenced by the United States, consistently disallows these efforts.[6]

In another sphere, more indirect but of enormous significance, are the huge subsidies for state-funded research and development. Astronomical sums have been allocated by the Pentagon—from the public's tax money—to underwrite technological developments. The fruits of these outlays—estimated at over *one trillion dollars* since 1945—among many others, have included the rapid development of computers and the fields of computer science and artificial intelligence. These industries and fields of study have contributed incalculably to U.S. ascendancy in information technology, computer networks, database creation, the special effects industry, and worldwide surveillance systems—the underlying infrastructure of what is now benignly termed "the information age." Without huge amounts of government money, this could not have happened.

Still another planned and direct state action to further U.S. communication primacy in the postwar years was the communication satellite undertaking. In this instance, the objective of this costly enterprise was explicit: It aimed to wrest global information control from America's "special partner," Great Britain, which up to that time had exercised worldwide domination of undersea cable. Testifying before Congress in 1966,

McGeorge Bundy, former chief aide to President Kennedy and
later president of the Ford Foundation, recollected, "I was
myself, a part of the executive branch during the period which
led up to the establishment of Comsat [Communication Satellite Corporation].... I do clearly remember what the record
fully confirms—that Comsat was established for the purpose
of taking and holding a position of leadership for the United
States in the field of international global commercial satellite
services."[7] The State Department's legal adviser at the time,
Mr. A. Chayes, was even more explicit. He noted that it was
the rapid growth of U.S. satellite technology in the 1950s that
undercut Britain's chance to extend control of cable communication for another several decades.[8]

In sum, the U.S. state has played a pivotal role in achieving
and maintaining American global cultural/informational domination over the last fifty years, a domination enduring to this
day. The effort has been fully conscious and deliberate, carried
out by each administration, from Truman's to Clinton's.

THE DISCONTINUITY FABLE
AND THE SURVIVAL OF HISTORY

In *Theories of the Information Society,* Frank Webster makes a
crucial distinction, in the study of contemporary communication theory, between those writers who see today's world as a
rupture with the past, and those who find "historical
antecedents and *continuities.*"[9] Webster comes down firmly on

the side of historical continuity. Yet his is by no means a majority view in recent times. In the postwar decades at least three variants of the rupture-of-history theory have had a powerful influence in fortifying the ideology of capitalism. One of the early expressions of this thinking came from Daniel Bell and those who took up his lead. Bell set the stage for what was to follow with his study of what he called post-industrial society.[10]

The appearance of a huge white-collar workforce, to which Bell gave prominent recognition, was taken by many interpreters to mean that the old industrial system, along with all its defining characteristics and institutions, was dead. The far-reaching restructuring of labor and industry could easily be pushed further—and it was—to conclude that a new age had emerged, one in which old forms and relations had disappeared. How this new social order differed from, but still related to the industrial system did not greatly concern the proponents of postindustrial society. Difference, yes! Connectedness, no! Writing about this disinclination, Dan Schiller noted, "Post-industrial theory utilized its exceptionalist premise [the uniqueness of 'information' and its production] to invoke a comprehensive but undemonstrable historical rupture, and therefore to draw back decisively from the predominating social relations of production and into schematic and false models of social development. 'Information' itself was given an aura of objectivity."[11]

The collapse of the Soviet Union, with the global "triumph" of United States capitalism that it signified, prompted a second version of a new age to be articulated. This was the thrust of *The*

End of History and the Last Man, in which Francis Fukuyama, to
the delight of those tired of confrontation and polarities, also
heralded a new era—one, according to the author, in which serious social conflict is absent, and a steady incrementalism toward
social improvement can be expected.[12] Fukuyama considered this
a boring but inevitable process.

In the postindustrial age, labor is seen as essentially unin-
volved in the social process because there is no need for
assertive labor. Labor's needs will be satisfied by the ongoing
process of social betterment driven by well-disposed pluralistic
forces. Inconveniently for this theory, the "benign" social
forces foreseen by Fukuyama are rapidly reversing the century-
long push toward greater social welfare. Triumphant capitalism
has unleashed a powerful drive toward inequality, not improvement, in the social sphere.

Today, therefore, the latest theory of historical rupture is
represented by the claims of the electronic crowd, who now
comprise a strident chorus. In this group may be included the
communication hardware and software people who speak
mostly with market expectations in mind. But there is also the
academic contingent, centered in the high-tech universities,
and most consequentially, political figures in the highest reaches
of the government.

One of the earliest proponents of the theory of a new electronic age, and its alleged break with the past, is Alvin Toffler.
In a series of books, beginning in 1970, which received mass
circulation and wide, national attention, Toffler breathlessly
described the computer-using society as the "third wave," dis-

placing the preceding industrial one that came, in turn, after the agricultural era.[13]

More recently, feverishly enthusiastic accounts of the networked age have been served up by *Wired* magazine, a monthly with a sizable readership. *Wired*'s editorial posture is to present itself and the material it publishes as bold, fresh, innovative, and indispensable for clues about what is happening in a culture undergoing digitization. According to *Wired*'s contributors and editors, we are on the threshold, if not already in, a new and wonderful world. The magazine's outlook, as described by an outsider, is that "computers lead to a kind of Utopia; a better future through symbiosis between man and machine… a religion that sees cyberspace as a transcendental medium which will usher in a Golden Age, an age where being digital frees the mind, allowing us to transcend the body and ascend to a higher plane of consciousness."[14]

When such a transcendental fantasy is accepted, on-the-ground problems that have endured since the beginning of industrialization—insecurity, poverty, unemployment, exploitation—fade from sight and consideration. The class struggle, for example, is transformed into an opposition between those who support and those who are unreceptive to the Internet.[15] Yet *Wired*, and the many other equally fervent media and academic voices claiming transformative power for electronic networks, are at most only a cheering section for processes under way that are energized by powerful political and economic forces. Far more influential in affecting actual developments in the restructuring of the economy is government—much maligned, incidentally, by *Wired* and other, now numerous, laissez-faire advocates in the country.

Federal initiatives and massive financial support for new communication technologies over the last half century have already been noted. This lavish underwriting of research and development for informational projects has scarcely diminished in the present digital period. To the contrary, communication has been elevated to a top government priority since the beginning of the Clinton administration in 1993. The president, and Vice President Gore, no less than *Wired* magazine, rhapsodize over the capability of the new information technologies to transform everyday life and to overcome the pervasive economic and social disabilities that scar modern existence.[16]

Yet Washington's view, no less exuberant than those of other electronic believers, retains of necessity an acknowledgment of history. This is so because in any period the exercise of power cannot overlook past experience. In the current American situation, a glance is in order back to 1941—the year in which Henry Luce proclaimed the advent of the American Century. In the late 1990s, a reconstituted American Century founded on electronic mastery has been contemplated.

This is the core of the argument that sees electronic communication and information as the guarantors of America's command of the world economy in the twenty-first century. One proponent from the computer software industry, Daniel F. Burton, Jr., vice president of government relations at Novell and the former president of the private-sector Council on Competitiveness, has this to say: "As the pioneer of the [networked] economy, the United States will play a defining role in how it develops. No other country combines the diverse set of assets necessary to drive its evolution—a towering software presence, a world-class hardware business, a dynamic content industry, a telecommunications sector that is rapidly being deregulated, a strong venture capitalist base, flexible labor markets, and an unparalleled university system." From this, Burton concludes, "It will be a networked world comprised of electronic communities of commerce and culture—a world that ironically will strengthen the position of the United States as a nation among nations, even as it disrupts the system of nation-states."[17]

This thinking comes close to being a blueprint of current U.S. strategic communication policy. President Clinton put it this way: "To keep the United States on the cutting edge, my job is to adjust America so we can win in the twenty-first century."[18] The government, no less than industry and happy, networked academics, confers on the new electronics a revolutionary role. Industry and university voices are more inclined to claim that the technology is producing a totally new world. The state and its administrators, more aware of power relations, nationally and globally, announce their intention to incorporate the new technologies into historically familiar structures of control and domination.

However strongly, therefore, the electronic faithful insist on the totality of difference the new instrumentation provides, the state authority matter-of-factly reveals the historical continuities in its quest for systemic power and control. The goal of electronic mastery fits smoothly into recognizable patterns of earlier imperial structures of privilege and exploitation.

This hardly escapes the attention of those most vulnerable to this power. The Canadian deputy prime minister, for example, openly challenged what she termed "American cultural imperialism" and stated that "if the Americans insist in pursuing their domination of the world culture community by using all the instruments at their disposal, they will expect the same in return."[19] Easier said than done!

EMERGENCE OF THE TRANSNATIONAL SYMBOLIC FACTORY: The Consequent Necessity for a Political Economy of Culture

Finally, what has been the culmination, to date, of the U.S. state's interventionist role in communication developments, and the denial of history in the ideological sphere? Can anyone still doubt the centrality of the communication (production) sector in the U.S. economy? In 1996, for example, two giant firms, Microsoft and Intel—one in software and the other in hardware—reported net profits that totalled $11 billion. This colossal return catapulted Intel into second place in the national corporate profitability scale, behind General Electric and ahead of Exxon. "In a sense," the report stated, "the duopoly is already the world's most successful commercial enterprise."[20]

Yet this is no aberrant example. The 1990s have seen an incredible systemwide concentration of capital, the communication/media sector in particular being at the forefront. In 1996, for example, "the volume of [all] mergers and acquisitions done worldwide... added up to $1 trillion... and more than $650 billion in the U.S."[21]

Growth through merger, consolidation, and capital expansion in the symbol-producing industries has been especially active. Time Warner and Disney-Capital Cities-ABC, two $20-billion-plus communication/cultural conglomerates manufacture, among other symbolic products, films, TV programs, books, magazines, and recordings. At the same time, their holdings extend to the circuits that disseminate these products—e.g. cable systems, TV networks, theme parks, and so on.

To understand the stakes involved, the returns to the *Star Wars* trilogy of films offer some perspective. Beyond the $1.3 billion in movie tickets sold, there were $500 million in video sales, $300 million in CD-ROM and video games, $1.2 billion in toys and playing cards, $300 million in clothes and accessories, and $300 million in books and comics.[22] Four billion dollars is hardly small change.

Accordingly, a few dozen hardware and software mega-corporations increasingly fill U.S. and global space with their manufactured symbolic products. How is this rationalized, if it is, by the cultural oligarchs? If the CEO of Time Warner, for example, were asked, "Don't you think there is a potential danger in having such an aggregation of cultural power, of so much media power, in the hands of one company?" he might reply, "Our subsidiary companies make their own decisions," implying that there is no such thing as centralized control.[23]

But this fails to take into account a fundamental law at work in a market system. Seemingly autonomous decision makers still have to bring in a profit. In ways that are not necessarily crudely interventionist or manipulative, they will fashion their media product to guarantee that profit. You don't need a cultural police in a market system. The market system acts as a "KGB," and it works very effectively.

Another example of the need for a political economy of culture is offered in the spectacle of a former secretary of state shilling for Disney. In October 1997 a short press report stated that Henry Kissinger, former secretary of state and longtime pooh-bah of the foreign policy establishment, had been hired as a consultant by the Walt Disney Company, one of the country's largest cultural/media conglomerates. What better indication of the fusion of economics, politics, and culture? "Michael Eisner, the chairman of Disney," the account notes, "has hired Mr. Kissinger as an adviser in the company's dealings with China.... Disney views China as a potentially powerful market for films, videos, company stores, and even a theme park. Accordingly, the call was made to Kissinger."[24]

The effect on the viewer, reader, or listener of the consumption of conglomeratized corporate cultural outputs cannot be explored here. Yet one conclusion seems indisputable. Just as cultural production, in its basic forms and relations, becomes increasingly indistinguishable from production in general, a political economy of culture—a rigorous examination of its production and its consumption—becomes an obligatory and vital site for research and analysis.

To ignore or minimize the value of this field of inquiry is to relinquish understanding of, and therefore the capability for resistance to, the latest crucially important terrain of capitalism. The political economy of cultural production and consumption is a core element in a twenty-first-century understanding of capitalism. This is especially so in this age of "triumphant capitalism." How else to begin to challenge its material and symbolic authority?

NOTES

1. Paul Craig Roberts, "Newt Should Keep His Eye on the Enemy: Big Government," *Business Week*, January 13, 1997, 26.

2. Herbert I. Schiller, *Communication and Cultural Domination*, (White Plains, N.Y.: International Arts and Sciences Press, 1976). One of the first critiques of the free flow doctrine was written by this author and published in *Le Monde Diplomatique* in September 1975.

3. *The New York Times*, November 29, 1944; *Editor and Publisher*, April 21, 1945.

4. *Department of State Bulletin* 14, no. 344 (1946): 160.

5. Thomas Guback, *The International Film Industry* (Bloomington: Indiana University Press, 1969).

6. Anthony De Palma, "Canada Gives Ground in a Border Dispute over Magazines, but the United States is not Satisfied," *The New York Times,* July 30, 1998.

7. Senate Subcommittee on Communications, *Progress Report on Space Communications, Hearings before the Senate Subcommittee on Communications*, 89th Cong., 2nd sess., August 10, 17, 18, and 23, 1966, 81.

8. House Committee on Government Operations, *Satellite Communications (Part 1): Hearings before the Committee on Government Operations*, 88th Cong., 2nd sess., 1964, 364, 360.

9. Frank Webster, *Theories of the Information Society* (London: Routledge, 1995), 217, emphasis in original.

10. Daniel Bell, *The Coming of Post-Industrial Society* (New York: Basic, 1973).

11. Dan Schiller, *Theorizing Communication: A History* (New York: Oxford University Press, 1996), 167, 169.

12. Francis Fukuyama, *The End of History and the Last Man* (New York: Free Press, 1992).

13. Alvin Toffler, *The Third Wave* (New York: William Morrow, 1980).

14. David S. Bennahum, "The Myth of Digital Nirvana," *Educom Review* 31, no. 5 (September/October 1996): 24–25.

15. John Perry Barlow, "The Powers That Were," *Wired*, September 1996, 197–199.

16. *The National Information Infrastructure: The Administration's Agenda for Action*, Washington, D.C., September 15, 1993. For a fuller critique, see Herbert I. Schiller, *Information Inequality* (New York: Routledge, 1996).

17. Daniel F. Burton Jr., "The Brave New Wired World," *Foreign Policy*, no. 106 (Spring 1997): 23–37.

18. John Markoff, "Clinton Proposes Changes in Policy to Aid Technology," *The New York Times*, February 23, 1993, 1.

19. Craig Turner, "Canadian Official Hints at Trade War on Hollywood," *Los Angeles Times*, February 11, 1997, 1.

20. Dean Takahashi, "Intel's Net Doubles on Overseas Demand," *Wall Street Journal*, January 15, 1997, A-3.

21. Steven Lipin, "Corporations' Dreams Converge in One Idea: It's Time to Do a Deal," *Wall Street Journal*, February 26, 1997, 1.

22. James Sterngold, "The Return of the Merchandiser," *The New York Times*, January 30, 1997, C-1.

23. Frank Rich reports in his *New York Times* column (March 6, 1997, A-19) that "the powers that be at NBC and ABC both said that their corporate bosses, Jack Welch and Michael Eisner respectively, stay out of programming."

24. B. Weinraub, "Disney Hires Kissinger," *The New York Times*, October 10, 1997, B-7.

CHAPTER TWO

VISIONS OF GLOBAL
ELECTRONIC MASTERY

What will be the shape and contours of the next thousand years? Of the next hundred years? This is beyond prediction. The actions and inactions of hundreds of millions of people and nearly 200 states, will affect what kind of world emerges in the time ahead.

But not all the participants in this unfolding drama have equal roles. Some will have greater influence than others on what the world looks like in the coming years. One country— the United States—by virtue of its economic, military, and informational/cultural strength enjoys primacy. This does not mean that whatever Washington wants, it gets. Constraints— and they are numerous—do impose limitations on the world's acknowledged sole superpower.

Still, primacy affords America's governing class possibilities and options not available to other states, even highly developed ones. How to maximize, therefore, its current condition of singular power continues to provoke argument in the highest reaches of the social order. At the governing level, few question the desirability of pursuing an "imperial policy," however euphemistically it is described. As the debate swirls around the best way of achieving and nurturing it, the discussants range from grand theorists to nuts-and-bolts practitioners.

THE THEORETICIANS

One of the "moderate" strategists puts it this way: "The aim of American foreign policy is to work with other like-minded actors to 'improve' the market place, to increase compliance with basic norms, by choice if possible, by necessity, i.e. coercion, if need be. At the core, regulation [of the international system] is an imperial doctrine in that it seeks to promote a set of standards we endorse, something not to be confused with imperialism, which is a foreign policy of exploitation."[1]

In this view, imperialism is defined as an exclusively European practice. Other American voices are less shy about using tougher terminology in prescribing America's current role in the world arena. Irving Kristol, a long-standing proponent of a belligerent conservatism, for example, shrugs off the notion of constraints and takes for granted an "emerging American imperium." (Note though that this more muscular approach is diffident about adopting the term imperialism.) "One of these days," Kristol writes, "the American people are going to awaken to the fact that we have become an imperial nation." He rushes to reassure his readers that this is no sought-after or intentional development. "It happened," he suggests, "because the world wanted it to happen." Elaborating this curious explanation, he notes that "a great power can slide into commitments without explicitly making them."[2]

Under his imperium, Kristol sees Europe embracing its dependence on the United States, and abdicating an independent foreign policy. "They [Europeans] are dependent nations, though they have a very large measure of local autonomy." Something akin, perhaps, to the Palestine Authority on the West Bank? Even such a staunch region of habitual resistance to United States intervention as Latin America, Kristol says, "is coming to recognize the legitimacy of U.S. leadership… and to [accept] a gradual Americanization of [its] popular culture and way of life."

Kristol himself is bemused by what he sees happening, and he distinguishes it from the older European imperialism, with its brutal, overt coercion. "Our missionaries," he writes, "live in Hollywood." Yet Kristol concludes on a bleak note: "It is an imperium with a minimum of moral substance. While the people of the world may want it and need it now, one wonders how soon they will weary of it."[3]

Kristol is among those who see U.S. global control as an unproblematic condition. Rivals are subduable by one means or another. Yet the view that is most influential in the American governing political class, up to now at least, expresses doubt that full political control, hegemony, can be achieved. Though completely at ease with the idea of a twenty-first American Century, it accepts the necessity of enlisting partners, however temporarily, in running the world and maintaining global order and discipline.

Unilateral action for these purposes, in this view, is risky and costly. It may be acceptable or necessary in extreme situations, but in general, soliciting support is preferable. Richard Haass, director of foreign studies at the Brookings Institution and formerly a special assistant to President George Bush, is a proponent of the currently prevailing view. He writes approvingly of the Persian Gulf War as a model for future policy.

In his book, imaginatively titled *The Reluctant Sheriff*, Haass recommends that the United States should be the global sheriff. He eschews the designation of policeman; his sheriff is more of a part-time worker. He comes to work when there is a demand to organize a raid on some recalcitrant powers, "rogue states" in Haass's lexicon, or—looked at differently—areas or groups that don't accept U.S.-imposed arrangements.

The sheriff assembles posses of "willing states" to be the enforcers. In this mainstream American view—the Brookings Institution is regarded as a "centrist" research body—a frontier species of vigilantism is advocated as foreign policy. How well a posse policy will fare in a world with 3 billion people below the poverty line and nuclear warheads scattered around a dozen or more regions like melons in a field, is not easy to imagine.

Underlying these strategic outlooks is an uncomplicated reading of the outcome of the Cold War: "We won, and the other side not only lost but disappeared."[4] With this interpretation in hand, the geopoliticians weave their imperial reveries.

THE PRACTITIONERS

More consequential perhaps are the blueprints, some already drafted, and the constructions they envisage for the material basis of the world economy in the immediate years to come. In this more practical realm, a loose, working coalition now exists of governmental, military, and business interests spanning the computer, media, and information industries. This group's vision has a decidedly electronic cast.

No less than the geostrategists, this grouping has its eyes focused on an American-directed world. It strongly insists that the means of achieving this is the electronically based information/media component that confers cultural and general power. Representatives of this outlook come from the top echelons of power. In 1996, for example, a former assistant secretary of defense and a former vice chairman of the Joint Chiefs of Staff, both having served in the early years of the first Clinton administration, wrote about what they considered "America's information edge," asserting that "the one country that can lead the information revolution will be more powerful than any other... [and] for the foreseeable future, that country is the United States." Voicing the view of the coalitionists who want partners for their posses, Nye and Owens, two traditional pundits, add, "Just as nuclear dominance was the key to coalition leadership in the old era, information dominance will be the key in the information age." This affords them a feeling of optimism about the future. "In truth, the twenty-first century, not the twentieth, will turn out to be the period of America's greatest preeminence. Information is the new coin of the inter national realm, and the United States is better positioned than any other country to multiply the potency of its hard and soft power resources through information."[5]

This is not a unique view. Another former Clinton administration official, David Rothkopf, recently managing director of Kissinger Associates, Henry's consulting firm, for example, is no less ebullient in his expectations of an information/cultural-based American Century. His essay "In Praise of Cultural Imperialism?" not only mentions the verboten word but revels in its applicability to the American scene. Rothkopf asserts that "for the United States, a central objective of an Information Age foreign policy must be to win the battle of the world's information flows, dominating the airwaves as Great Britain once ruled the seas." Like Nye and Owens, he is confident that this will occur: "Inevitably, the United States... [is] the 'indispensable nation' in the management of global affairs and the leading producer of information products in these, the early years of the Information Age." Accordingly, he views current trends with satisfaction: "it is in the economic and political interests of the United States to ensure that if the world is moving to a common language, it be English; that if the world is moving toward common telecommunications, safety, and quality standards, they be American; that if the world is becoming linked by television, radio, and music, the programming be American; and that if common values are being developed, they be values with which Americans are comfortable."[6]

These "are not simply aspirations," Rothkopf observes, but

developing realities. "The realpolitik of the Information Age is that setting technological standards, defining software standards, producing the most popular information products, and leading in the related development of the global trade in services are as essential to the well-being of any would-be leader as once were the resources needed to support empire or industry." Finally, in laying out an information-based design for U.S. global ascendancy, Rothkopf gives a modest assessment of why everyone is bound to benefit from this plan. "...Americans should not deny the fact," he writes, "that of all the nations in the history of the world, theirs is the most just, the most tolerant, the most willing to constantly reassess and improve itself, and the best model for the future."

PRESIDENTIAL ENDORSEMENT OF THE ELECTRONIC VISION

Fantasy-ridden and arrogant as this interpretation may be, it is matched by Washington policy prescriptions—the nuts and bolts—in the information sphere. The high-tech information initiatives of the Clinton White House are dedicated unapologetically to keeping the United States numero uno in the global arena.

From the beginning of his presidency, President Clinton has had a close (fund-raising, at the very least) connection to the electronics industry in Silicon Valley. Vice President and presidential candidate Al Gore has been presented as a fan of computers. He has surrounded himself with electronics executives. "Once a month," it is reported, "Vice President Al Gore meets privately with a select group of Silicon Valley entrepreneurs." The topics, the account states, "vary from month to month, but the overarching agenda is the same: fathoming the implications of America's 'new economy,' and devising practical solutions to public policy problems large and small." One of the participants in the meetings confesses: "We're so conceited that we think what's in the best interest of our industry is in the best interest of the whole country."[7]

This evokes memories of "Engine Charlie" Wilson, General Motors' chief in World War II days, who blithely tied the country's welfare to GM's profits. In the late 1990s, however, such a sentiment has appropriately expressed and described national policy. Government has led the march into the electronic age. In its rhetoric and in its actions it has insisted that full computerization of the economy is imperative for national growth and for global ascendancy. Understandably, the communications industry has no trouble in agreeing.

In the last few years, the project for a wired country and a networked world has moved from blueprint to near reality. Announced with presidential authority in September 1993, the proposed National Information Infrastructure (NII) was presented as the all-inclusive electronic answer to whatever ailed the country, as well as the means to provide for the improvement and enrichment of the human race.[8] The benefits were enumerated with unqualified enthusiasm: round-the-clock communication for the family; education online from the best teachers in the country; access to global resources of art, literature, and science; health services for all online, with no waiting; working at home; the latest entertainment in your living room; easy access to government officials and all kinds of online information. Yet one central stipulation accompanied these for the most part ambiguous benefits, a proviso that over time, could only negate the promised benefits. The NII's foundation statement was most explicit. "The private sector," it was mandated, "will lead the deployment of the NII.... Businesses [are] responsible for creating and operating the NII."[9]

And so this remarkable information technology, initially developed with government money and operated as a public utility, was handed to a clutch of powerful corporate communication corporations—computer makers, software designers, telecommunications providers, and media producers—for its development and expansion. The corporate communication industry has responded to these new and potentially rewarding opportunities with a frenzied merger and concentration movement, piling resources and capital into enormous companies. There has also been a rash of governmental auctions of the radio spectrum to the telecommunications giants, in preparation for the expanded services that the new spectrum holders will deem profitable.

Here too public property—the airwaves—has with no debate been removed from social accountability and released to those whose commercial interests are inherently incompatible with community requirements. With these material conditions secured, and private communications giants primed and encouraged to exploit to the fullest the emerging digital networks, the latest governmental intervention on their behalf took up the crucial issue of markets, mostly foreign ones.

THE FRAMEWORK FOR
GLOBAL ELECTRONIC COMMERCE

The release of a White House–drafted document, *The Framework for Global Electronic Commerce*, in July 1997, urged the unrestricted flow of electronic commerce, domestically and internationally.[10] This recommended statement of policy noted the already substantial use of the National Information Infrastructure (NII) and the Global Information Infrastructure (GII). It pointed out that "world trade involving computer software, entertainment products (motion pictures, videos, games, sound recordings), information services (databases, online newspapers), technical information, product licences, financial services, and professional services (business and technical consulting, accounting, architectural design, legal advice, travel services, etc.) has grown rapidly in the past decade, now accounting for well over $40 billion of U.S. exports alone," and that "an increasing share of these transactions occurs online."

It is expected that this commerce will expand rapidly in the years ahead. The International Telecommunications Union (ITU), for example, reported that the Internet "has been doubling in size every year for the past decade… [and] by the year 2000 there are likely to be some 110 million host computers connected to the Internet, implying a user base of around 300 million."[11] It is this present and future global market that is the central concern of the *Framework* paper. The latter's advocacy of free-flowing electronic commerce would seem an unexceptional, indeed welcome development if there were numerous participants, more or less evenly matched, in the domestic and international arenas.

The reality is otherwise. The emerging electronic economy, in one crucial respect, resembles the situation in the immediate post–World War II days. At that time, the United States emerged unscathed and more powerful than any combination of rivals. As mentioned, it demanded and enforced a "free flow of information," which enabled the American media/cultural corporate giants to blanket the world with their products and services. This policy has prevailed over the last half century, actively promoted and supported by a variety of U.S. governmental instruments: foreign aid, subsidies, economic pressure on potential recalcitrants, and many varieties of political arm-twisting. As a result, made-in-America cultural and informational outputs, and the English language, now dominate movie and TV screens, music making, entertainment centers, and business conversation.[12]

But the technological underpinning of the American industrial state has undergone a massive transformation since the end of World War II. The computerization and digitization of the economy has proceeded apace. Industries that didn't exist fifty years ago have grown spectacularly, spawning some of the most powerful corporate enterprises in the world, e.g. Intel, Microsoft, Compaq, and so on. The production and sale of information have also become major businesses, as have the telecommunications companies that carry the streams of information (data, messages, and images) operating globally, increasingly in linkups and alliances with foreign carriers.

These developments and others comprise what is commonly called "globalization." Actually, this is a misleading term, falsely giving the impression that everything has become globalized. The main constituents of globalization are the big corporations—in automobiles, oil, consumer goods, banking, and financial electronic services—and their increasingly transnational operations. It is on their behalf and in their interest that the current policy making of the United States, Japan, and Europe is formulated. Some coordination among these groupings occurs to provide a measure of stability and security for the globe-girdling activities of the transnational system at large, and each nation's home-based enterprises in particular.

Ultimately, each transnational firm strives for its own advantage, and is supported in that effort by the state power wherein it resides, or at least where its main shareholders are domiciled. The power that a nation or regional grouping, such as Europe, can bring to bear in support of its national enterprises is a function of that political entity's generalized strength—economically, militarily, culturally. By this criterion, the United States continues to be in a class by itself.

This is the context in which the *Framework for Global Electronic Commerce* emerges. It is, in short, a preemptive statement, intended to organize the digital age according to rules most helpful to its formulator, the United States. These rules will enforce the already considerable advantages the American communication industries now possess against existing or potential rivals. Once more, this effort is couched in the language of freedom.

"Commerce on the Internet," the document states, "could total tens of billions of dollars by the turn of the century." This can only eventualize, the statement cautions, under certain conditions. "For this potential to be realized fully," the *Framework* draft insists, "governments must adopt a non-regulatory, market-oriented approach to electronic commerce, one that facilitates the emergence of a transparent and predictable legal environment to support global business and commerce."

The danger, as the U.S. policy statement sees it, is "that some governments will impose extensive regulations on the Internet and electronic commerce." What might some of these restrictions be? "Potential areas of problematic regulation" are seen to "include taxes and duties, restrictions on the type of information transmitted, control over standards development, licensing requirements, and rate regulation of service providers."

Manifestly, the *Framework* document is written to preclude actions that a sovereign state might want to take either to protect its economic viability and independence or to challenge arrangements established by the controllers of the system—standards, licensing, rate regulation, and so on. Most fundamental of all, *The Framework* prescribes the social basis of those states agreeing to abide by its principles: whether the economy should be socially or privately structured, for example, is not an option.

The document is unambiguous about this: "governments should encourage industry self-regulation wherever appropriate and support the efforts of private sector organizations to develop mechanisms to facilitate the successful operation of the Internet." It follows that the new electronic commerce policy rejects the regulatory framework established over the last sixty years for telecommunications, radio, and television, in a period in which public interest protections were mandated and social needs were acknowledged, if not heeded, in the operative policies.

In the 1990s, a time of corporate capital's global ascendancy, the mildest restraints on its prerogatives have been peremptorily rejected. Automatically, under this designation, measures to protect national cultural industries, for example, have been ruled unacceptable infringements of "free trade." Informational and cultural creations have been made indistinguishable from commercial goods and have been treated as such. This meshes nicely with the needs of American cultural conglomerates, but it is not exactly a popular idea in many parts of the world. Only the strength of the U.S. economy, and the threat of closing its huge market to recalcitrant states, overcomes most opposition.

The stakes already are considerable.[13] Moreover, the White House quotes projections of electronic commerce "growing to more than $300 billion in just a few years."[14] Free flow of electronic commerce may be the policy of the American cultural industries and their Washington representatives, but at the same time no effort is being spared to ensure that this commerce is not "free" in the customary sense of the word.

It is in this context that the issue of intellectual property has risen to a new prominence. A genuine free flow of information would suggest a loosening of intellectual property laws and an increased general and free accessiblity to creative work wherever it appeared. Far from it. Lester Thurow, a sometimes populist economist, explains the new situation: "Intellectual property lies at the center of the modern company's economic success or failure.... Increasingly, intellectual property is becoming central to strategic battle plans."

Thurow sees the emerging digital period following a historical progression: "The Industrial Revolution began with an enclosure movement that abolished common land in England. The world now needs a socially managed movement for intellectual property rights, or it will witness a scramble among the powerful to grab valuable pieces of intellectual property, just as the powerful grabbed the common lands of England three centuries ago."[15]

What we are witnessing, in fact, *is* a corporate enclosure of intellectual property, a process that hardly can be called "socially managed." Intellectual property rights are being strengthened and extended, and new means devised to ensure that these rights cannot be breached. One author, looking into the near future, inquires, "What will the act of reading be like if every time I open a book I must negotiate the terms under which I read it?"[16]

Most of this activity is justified by the once-valid notion of protecting the rights of individual creators-authors-designers-artists-filmmakers, and to provide continuing incentives for their creative work. Though such individual work continues, the larger share of intellectual-artistic creation today is produced under corporate auspices, with the individual talent and skills under contract to huge research and cultural factories. Individual incentives in this environment are laughable.

The big publishers, conglomeratized film and TV producers, and corporate research labs are intent that their outputs, which they want to circulate on the Internet, are easily available *but not for free.* To this end, relief and joy were expressed when "digital object identifiers" were unveiled at the Frankfurt Book Fair in October 1997. "It's one of the most important events in publishing for this century, and I don't think I'm saying too much," the chief executive of Axel Springer Verlag, the German publishing giant, explained.[17]

This awkwardly named technology is an electronic branding technique that enables intellectual property to be numbered, identified, and monitored as it hurtles through cyberspace, thus guaranteeing that it will not be appropriated without some specified payment. It is one of the many ways, and an important one, that the Internet may be transformed into a predominantly commercial venue, rather than a public commons.

In the emerging digital era, the corporate owners of intellectual property hope to charge for any and all use of their holdings. The flow of electronic "commerce"—which now includes human and social creativity—will be sold in domestic and global markets, at the same time that older forms of social usage, i.e. "fair use," are limited if not eliminated, and another pillar of social public space crumbles. The free flow of electronic commerce, in concert with strengthened intellectual property rights, constitutes the underpinning of the new global corporate information order.

The *Framework* statement invokes the First Amendment to the U.S. Constitution as the essential grounding for the free flow of information, which it seeks to extend as a global principle. In fact the First Amendment was intended to protect individual speech, not corporate expression. The U.S. Constitution is being invoked to serve as the protection of corporate messages and images.

When this willful confusion is permitted to exist, as it is in the United States today, efforts to protect the public against plutocratically financed expression are prevented. This is even more so in the international sphere, where nations, to the extent that they accept a corporate definition of free flow of information, are deprived of their cultural and often political sovereignty.

It is, in fact, actions that might be taken by states defending their autonomy that are the concern of Washington and their constituents in the high-tech corporate communication sector. Accordingly, taxes and tariffs on the Internet, threats to copyright protection for motion pictures, computer software, and sound recordings disseminated via the GII, security of database and patent holdings—all the forms of property in an information age—are worrisome to the new property holders.

The Framework sternly states, "The legal framework supporting commercial transactions on the Internet should be governed by consistent principles across state, national, and international borders that lead to predictable results regardless

of the jurisdiction in which a particular buyer or seller resides."
With this proposal seemingly fair-minded, yet oblivious to disparities and inequalities between states and regions and peoples,
the interests of powerful corporate intellectual property holders
take precedence over the weaker partners in the transactions.

In this crucial respect, *The Framework for Global Electronic
Commerce* represents an extension of the post–World War II
free flow of information doctrine to the digital age. It comes at
a time when the American electronic advantage over other
states is enormous. For example, "The worldwide breakdown
of the number of personal computers connected to the Internet may be summarized as follows: the United States,
10,110,000 computers, for 62.6 percent of the total; Japan,
730,000 computers, 4.5 percent; Germany, 720,000 computers, 4.5 percent, Canada, 600,000 computers, 3.7 percent; and
the United Kingdom, 590,000 computers, 3.7 percent."[18]
These figures undoubtedly will change over time, but they
demonstrate the mid-1997 world distribution of electronic
capability. The United States intends to consolidate, by one
means or another, its present superiority. The free flow of
information doctrine is one such means.

"The U.S. government," the *Framework* paper states,

> supports the broadest possible free flow of information
> across international borders. This includes most infor-
> mational material now accessible and transmitted
> through the Internet, including through World Wide
> Web pages, news and other information services, virtual

shopping malls, and entertainment features, such as radio and video products, and the arts. This principle extends to information created by commercial enterprises as well as by schools, libraries, governments, and other nonprofit entities.

The free flow of information doctrine, undeniably beneficial to the already powerful, is a fraudulent construct. The flow of information it promotes is free in one respect only. The flow is expected to be freely admitted to all the spaces that its providers desire to transmit it to. Otherwise, there is nothing free about the information. Quite the contrary. Information and message flows are already, and will continue to be, priced to exact the highest revenues extractable. Recent decades have witnessed the steady transformation of public information into saleable goods. Improved electronic information processing facilitates greatly the ability to package and charge for all kinds of messages and images.

The *Framework* paper is explicit about its concern with proprietary information. A major section of the paper is devoted to carefully enumerating the means and needs for electronic payment systems. "New technology," it notes, "has made it possible to pay for goods and services over the Internet." This demands "international agreements that establish clear and effective copyright, patent, and trade mark protection."

Still, it is necessary to recognize that the *Framework* document represents intentions, not currently implementable policy. It is a first initiative—a second was announced on November 30,

1998, reaffirming the document—from Washington, to secure a lion's share of the world market for the growing flow of electronic commerce, originating largely from the operational activities of transnational companies. Its strictures against regulation, at least for the domestic economy, cannot be taken at face value. The Clinton administration's endorsement of encryption controls, for example, is hardly compatible with its insistence on a nonregulatory environment of the Internet. This was pointed out by the *New York Times* reporter on information issues, John Markoff. The proposed encryption legislation circulated by the White House, Markoff observes, "appears to contradict the administration's support for unregulated development on the Internet."[19]

But the contradiction is easily resolved. The *Framework* draft is not intended for the domestic sphere. Though its language contains the usual anti-regulation rhetoric, governmental practices in the information sector for fifty years consistently belie the ritualistic exhortations on behalf of a free market. Internationally, it's a different story.

As Columbia University professor Eli Noam perceptively writes, "A close reading of the [*Framework*] report does not indicate a move by the federal government toward lessened economic regulation of those things it cares about. The report's ringing language is hence largely directed at efforts by other governments—states and other countries—to impose economic regulation on the Internet."[20]

This is the familiar routine of telling others what to do while ignoring that advice in one's own actions. How well it can or will succeed is not entirely a matter of U.S. will and its present electronic primacy. Long-term American mastery of cyberspace is neither predestined nor guaranteed. National wills can intervene to press for alternative outcomes.

In the short term, the economic power of transnational capital, and the extent to which a people have been exposed to and have accepted the multimedia marketing environment on which the American economy is based, will give support to Washington's electronic reveries. So too will U.S. military power, fortified with advanced communication technology and deployed to surveil and intervene anywhere across the globe. "The message," the recent chief of the U.S. Atlantic Command says, "is that there is no nation on the face of the earth that we cannot get to."[21]

For the more distant time, however, the wild imbalances that this system of unaccountable corporate/military power imposes on people and resources will produce intensifying shocks that may throw the entire enterprise into calamitous disarray.

NOTES

1. Richard N. Haass, *The Reluctant Sheriff* (New York: Council on Foreign Relations, 1997), 70.

2. Irving Kristol, "The Emerging American Imperium," *Wall Street Journal,* August 18, 1997, A-14.

3. Ironically, a study of the global media, written from a totally different perspective, is subtitled "The Global Missionaries of Corporate Capitalism," Edward Herman and Robert McChesney, *The Global Media* (London: Cassell, 1997).

4. Haass, *Reluctant Sheriff,* 56.

5. Joseph S. Nye, Jr. and William A. Owens, "America's Information Edge," *Foreign Affairs*, March/April 1996, 20–36.

6. David Rothkopf, "In Praise of Cultural Imperialism?", *Foreign Policy*, no. 107, (Summer 1997): 38–53.

7. Elizabeth Shogren, "Gore Finds Brain Trust in Silicon Valley Group," *Los Angeles Times*, August 25, 1997, 1.

8. National Information Infrastructure (NII), *Agenda for Action*, September 15, 1993, Washington, D.C.

9. Ibid.

10. *The Framework for Global Electronic Commerce*, The White House, Washington, D.C., July 1, 1997. Announced by President Clinton and Vice President Gore.

11. "A Global View of Internet's Rise," *New York Times*, September 8, 1997.

12. *The New York Times Magazine*, June 7, 1997.

13. George Anders, "Click and Buy," *Wall Street Journal*, December 7, 1998, R-4.

14. *The Framework for Global Electronic Commerce*.

15. L. Thurow, "Needed: A New System of Intellectual Property Rights," *Harvard Business Review*, September/October 1997, 95–103.

16. Charles C. Mann, "Who Will Own Your Next Good Idea?" *Atlantic Monthly*, 282, no. 3 (September 1998): 82.

17. Doreen Carvajal, "Electronic Branding Receives Accolades at the Frankfurt Book Fair," *The New York Times*, October 20, 1997, C-11.

18. "Communications in Japan 1997 (White Paper)," *New Breeze* (Tokyo), Summer 1997, 19.

19. John Markoff, "Law Proposed to Regulate Devices that Code Messages," *The New York Times*, September 7, 1997, 14.

20. Eli Noam, "Why the Internet will be Regulated," *Educom Review* 32, no. 5 (September/October 1997): 12–14.

21. Hugh Pope, "U.S. Plays High-Stakes War Games in Kazakstan," *Wall Street Journal*, September 16, 1997, A-16.

CHAPTER THREE

COMMUNICATION TODAY: WHAT'S NEW?

The world capitalist system that the United States labors to oversee has been transformed in recent decades. In the many changes that have occurred, a few features stand out.

There is visibly and palpably a gargantuan concentration of capital, best illustrated by, but by no means exclusive to, the United States. The corporate sector, which in pre–World War II years already was a dominating presence, came out of the war a behemoth. There is simply no comparing, for example, a General Electric with current assets in the hundred billions with its prewar status. The process has not been concluded, and the pyramidization of assets proceeds feverishly. The outcome, unable to be predicted with specificity, cannot fail to produce a handful of global economic giants in the various sectors of the world economy.

In the communication sphere, this concentration has been occurring at an intensifying tempo over the last twenty years, driven by a gale of new technologies and, more importantly, by the systemic requirements of the transnational corporate order, which is heavily reliant on communication for its global operations and its worldwide marketing efforts. It follows that new investments in telecommunications have become significant percentages of the economy's total investment, and that the communication sector has become the pacemaker of the entire economy.

This enhanced corporate sphere has focused its attention, in its drive for ever greater profitability, on the destruction of the state's social services activity and role, created during the Great Depression of the 1930s and expanded briefly in the 1960s. Confident of its growing strength, capital is no longer willing to accept limitations, especially those placed on it during earlier crisis times. It is more dismissive still of social measures aimed at alleviating the distress of that part of the population discarded or unutilized by the business system.

The banner of capital, in its push toward total social unaccountability, proclaims "deregulation." With deregulation, one sector of the economy after another is "liberated" to capital's unmonitored authority. The very notion that there is a public interest is contested. Public functions are weakened or eliminated. This occurs in most industrial states, at varying speeds, with minimum resistance. Opposition, where it develops, as in France in 1995, seems to be fighting a delaying action. The rampaging juggernaut of transnational capital is abetted by the powerful cultural industries and especially the mass media.

A modest case in point comes from the publishing field. A new economics text, anticipated to be the most widely adopted textbook in American universities and colleges in 1997, offers this perspective of current economic activity. The author "teaches that increases in government spending crowd out private capital, producing higher interest rates. Higher thrift and greater savings produce lower interest rates and higher economic growth. Unemployment is caused not by greedy industrialists, but by minimum wage laws, collective bargaining, unemployment insurance and other regulations that raise the cost of labor."[1]

This new primer, *Business Week* notes, "will play a big role in shaping public opinion about how the economy works."[2] It will also inform the new generation that the general efforts of working people to improve their lives over the last two centuries have been misguided. It will claim that the dismantlement of social protection is liberatory. And it will insist that the "principles of economics" it presents have universal applicability.

Deregulation and concentration of capital have been facilitated by the stream of new information technologies—many derived from America's enormous Cold War expenditures on military research and development. These technologies, beyond their obvious military purposes, have served the operational needs of transnational capital, as it undertakes production and distribution in multitudinous global sites. Vast electronic and telecommunications networks have been organized that are indispensable to corporate global activities. The circuits serve also to open up new markets and transmit, along with business data, the cultural products, and especially the advertising, of global companies. The combination of deregulation of industry, concentration of capital, and worldwide instantaneous communication is the essential pillar of a massive globalization of capital in recent decades. It is also the source of the ever-diminishing power of the nation-state, excluding only for the time being the most powerful nation-state, the United States.

The globalization of capital also serves as the battering ram that relentlessly attacks working people's living standards. And it is especially ruthless to national efforts of social protection. Though some still see the Internet, for example, as a democratic structure for international individual expression, it is more realistic to recognize it as only the latest technological vehicle to be turned, sooner or later, to corporate advantage—for advertising, marketing and general corporate aggrandizement.

The recently concluded merger of Netscape and America Online (AOL), a software producer and the major online provider, confirms this appraisal, and in fact, it has been reported this way: "By moving quickly toward what both companies have recently come to see as the inevitable convergence of technology and media, America Online hopes that it will secure a solid lead in a battle already joined by giants like the Microsoft Corporation and the International Business Machines Corporation (IBM) to transform the greater part of cyberspace into a vast virtual mall."[3]

Today the increasingly integrated communication system in most parts of the world is firmly in the hands of big capital. Capital investments in telecommunications, for example, run into the hundreds of billions of dollars annually. It is a system in which investment and production decisions are made less and less by national figures and more and more by transnational corporations and investors and their global institutions, such as the World Bank, the International Monetary Fund (IMF), the World Trade Organization (WTO), and so on. Some of the effects of the corporate control of communication are already manifest.

CAPITAL'S INSATIABILITY: The Takeover of Public Property and Services

What is becoming increasingly clear is the fierce and insatiable drive of capital to roll back as many as possible of the social measures that have been struggled for over the last two centuries. All of the tales of a reformed capitalism, a capitalism with a human face, a people's capitalism, have been repudiated. As vast new pools of labor from Russia, India, China, Indonesia, and the rest of the poor world enter the world economy, the balance between labor and capital, never equal in the past, becomes grossly tilted in favor of capital. New communication technologies enable the world business system to dip into these new reserves of labor power, to the great disadvantage of working people in the already industrialized and, at least partially, unionized labor force.

In this wildly out-of-alignment distribution of power, every social or public space or activity is either appropriated for commodity production and profitability or, failing that, left to wither away. In the United States, for example, the public school system is under siege, and various schemes to privatize schooling are treated with respect and credulity in the mass media. The progressive income tax, adopted more than eighty years ago after strong popular demand, is all but a memory. The people's political representatives talk of substituting blatantly regressive taxes, such as the flat tax or sales tax, for what remains of the income tax.

To those who regard any publicly supported activity as unacceptable, the arts are also in the target zone. The National Endowment for the Arts has been under constant attack, and its never-adequate budget has been reduced to a meager handout.

Another feature of unrestrained capital's onslaught is less visible, but no less threatening to a democratic order. The ongoing transfer of social services into for-sale transactions, if unchecked, will leave people comprehensively enmeshed in market relationships, losing further remnants of their communality. The private, for-pay child care center run by a corporate chain is another instance of this growing phenomenon.[4] Health care too has become, in the language of the day, "a profit center." Imagine, for-profit hospitals! Yet these are not fanciful projects. They exist and expand.

Then there is the press itself, a private institution from the beginning, in the West, at least. Freedom of the press is defined —by the press, naturally—as based on the private ownership of the press properties. This definition has been made part of the sacred texts of American capitalism, and no less so in Great Britain.

With this elemental grounding of the press, there has never been a mystery about which side—labor's or capital's—the media have been on. They are capital. But in the age of voracious capitalism, the managers and directors of the press—newspapers, radio, and television—go one step further. Now, the alleged age-old separation of editorial and business departments is being scrapped. The media are unashamedly offering their news and content to big advertisers and sponsoring corporations for review. What was once a variably nuanced management perspective has become full obeisance. This overt aggression against reliable information is reported in different accounts, of which the following is representative: "The *Los Angeles Times* announced a big step in its much-debated reorganization today. Its editor, Shelby Coffee III, resigned and the newspaper named a new editorial team that will further dismantle the wall that has traditionally separated the news and business sides at most major newspapers."[5] Perhaps the one positive aspect of this development is that it makes obvious and explicit a previously unacknowledged condition.

The concentration of capital reaches its apogee in the communication sector of the economy, and a no-holds-barred atmosphere permits the creation of giant cultural/media/communication predators. These have led a monumental looting of the public domain. The radio spectrum, that part of the physical universe that offers the frequencies to transmit radio, television, and other signals, has been the latest target of the privatizers and capital accumulators. From their earliest use, the airwaves were recognized as inalienable public property, no less a part of the national patrimony than air and water, and later, national parks and lands.

No longer. In a series of auctions, wide chunks of the spectrum have been sold off to telecommunications corporations, who already own the circuitry of the country's information system. Under previous arrangements, parts of the spectrum were given free of charge to broadcasting interests, but always with the proviso that ultimate control and disposition were vested in the state. Even if in reality the supervisory agency, the Federal Communications Commission (FCC), left matters in the hands of the private spectrum holders, the principle, if not the practice, of accountability remained in place.

Sale of the spectrum, however, removes that ultimate social authority and confers on the new owners property rights in perpetuity. The unwillingness of unleashed corporate enterprise to acknowledge any limits either to its demands or to its efforts to eliminate social space is a distinctive feature of post–Cold War capitalism.

DISAPPEARANCE OF THE THIRD WORLD

Another characteristic of this new age is the literal disappearance of what used to be called "the Third World." The poor, ex-colonial states have metamorphosed, under the spell and blandishments of Wall Street investors, into "emerging markets." What formerly were struggling, mostly unindustrialized states have become the locus of huge investment flows from the capital-rich nations of Western Europe, the United States, and Japan.

The leaders of these nations, left few practical alternatives by the demise of the Soviet system, have opted, some enthusiastically, others reluctantly, for the American "model"—privatization of their main industries, especially communication; concessions to foreign capital; and opening of commerce and culture to free trade and the free flow of information.

Third World demands expressed twenty-five years ago, for a new international economic and a new international information order, have been interred. There *is* a new economic and information order; but it is one that instead of conferring equity, reciprocity, and redistribution—the earlier objectives—imposes inequality, enrichment of a new, limited middle class, huge profits for the ownership stratum, domestic and foreign, and harsh working conditions for those employed. For the rest, a very sizeable portion of the population, there is continuing deep impoverishment. The model is on view on all continents.

No less a source than the *Wall Street Journal* informs us of the Mexican experience: "The Fund [International Monetary Fund] and the U.S. Administration keep bragging about the Mexican model.... After two years Mexico is now growing again in peso terms, but what the braggarts seldom note is that every Mexican worker took a 50 percent pay cut in world purchasing power terms, that inflation decimated the rising middle class, and that political instability is now on the uptick."[6]

A similar assessment could be made for Indonesia, Russia, Venezuela, and countless other impoverished states, whose resources have been plundered by small groups of domestic and foreign interests.

In Latin America, Mexico, Brazil, Argentina, and Chile are given special attention. In Asia, until the recent financial collapse in Thailand and across the area, South Korea, Indonesia,

Malaysia, Thailand, and China were viewed as especially attrac
tive areas for capital investment. Before the 1998 meltdown,
Eastern Europe—the Czech Republic, Hungary, Poland, and
Russia itself—got high marks from transnational corporations
and international investors. Washington, London, Paris, Tokyo,
and most of all Wall Street found these areas attractive sites for
their speculative capital flows.

Yet beyond the flashy expenditures of the new and modest-
sized consuming classes, the creation of a wrenching economic
and social divide characterizes each of these societies. Not only
do the earlier poverty and social distress endure and deepen,
but the new model brings with it all the cultural control mechanisms of its progenitors, the United States.

A quarter of a century ago, the ex-colonial states and other
poor nations sought an information order that would allow
diversity, openness, mutuality, and diminished commercialization and monopolistic control of cultural creation. Today the
"emerging markets" are swamped with the cultural/media
outputs of the Western cultural industries. The very notion of
cultural autonomy has disppeared into the maw of free trade
and market imperatives.

Turkey's experience, for example, is hardly unique. "How,"
asks a *Wall Street Journal* report, "did Philip Morris Co. capture
nearly a quarter of the cigarette market in Turkey, a nation
almost synonymous with tobacco?" Good question. The
answer: It used a "battle plan" that it "has perfected [in] setting
up operations in nearly thirty countries worldwide." This battle plan included such strategies as heavy lobbying to change

Turkey's laws; massive use of door-to-door salespeople; and "an advertising blitz."[7] The result was a weak country overwhelmed by a global corporate offensive.

Replacing the quest for a free, balanced, noncommercial information flow is the creation of satellite transmissions and digital networks, more dominated than ever by a few transnational corporate groups. Paradoxically, these technologies are promoted, and accepted, as advanced means to escape backwardness and impoverishment.

THE FUSION OF CULTURAL/SYMBOLIC PRODUCTION AND THE GENERAL ECONOMY

Another feature of contemporary capitalism is its enfolding of cultural/symbolic production into the systemic core. The expansion of the cultural-communication industries has become critical to the functioning of a globalized market economy. Media, publishing, advertising, public relations, opinion polling, accounting, consultancy, and market research today constitute an essential protective ring around the activities of the goods and services production center.

The transnational corporate drive for markets is dependent on the use of saturation advertising in targeted areas. Opinion polling affords political governors the capability to monitor minutely the sentiments of their people, enabling the appropriate public relations to be applied to the problems at hand, be they elections, corruption, or military adventures.

A local example is illustrative. The city of San Diego in

southern California is located in an arid region. At the same time it is profligate in its use of water. Now a shortage looms. The city leaders are proposing a purification plant that will take sewage and transform it into drinkable water. Most people are revolted by the idea. The first step, therefore, in this undertaking is to hire a public relations firm to persuade the citizens that the proposal is safe and satisfactory. "Even before it has started building the waste-water recycling plant, the city has spent more than $2 million to hire a public relations firm, conduct public outreach meetings and set up briefing sessions and hot lines."[8] As Daniel Lerner would have put it, the governing process now avails itself of "enlightenment" as a substitute for coercion.

Not surprisingly, these somewhat newly developed fields are staffed with the most highly trained and capable members of the labor force. They have quickly become an important element of governing power. The film and television industries, important since their inception as providers of popular diversion and the dominant ideology, have become economic heavyweights as well, exporting billions of dollars' worth of symbolic product, second only to the exports of the aerospace industry.

Domestically, we are overwhelmed by a continuous barrage of commercial messages, trivial news broadcasts, and endless sports programming. Watching television, it seems that America is made up of models, celebrities, grasping politicians, and athletes. Along with the Third World, working people are nearly totally absent. Still, it must be emphasized that this arsenal of communication services at the disposal of the controllers is by no means a guarantee of frictionless stability. It aims at this condition, but it cannot overcome numerous and unexpected sources of resistance.

CONCLUSION

The international communication field that was the subject of intense dispute thirty years ago is still recognizable. Despite astonishing technological developments, industrial concentration and mergers, new global alliances, and additional communication voices, the world information order remains for the large part still American.

Cyberspace has been added to familiar communication terrain, but the transmitters with few exceptions continue to be corporate voices, mostly from a handful of countries. Advertising more than ever remains the fount that finances much of the global media cultural flow. There are more subcenters of media and data production, but ultimately they are subordinate to the central producers. And, more evident today than before, there is not one medium of domination but a multimedia/multicommunications facility enterprise, horizontally and vertically integrated.

With deregulation imposed across all continents, the state retains less ability to intervene and socially manage the system. A worldwide capitalist presence in all cultural/media space grows apace, squeezing out the social sphere. Will this process reach its ultimate destination—a form of global corporate feudalism? The jury—six billion people—is still to be heard from.

NOTES

1. Mark Skousen, "Keynesianism Defeated," *Wall Street Journal,* October 9, 1997.

2. P. Coy, "Let's Not Take Feel-Good Economics Too Far," *Business Week,* October 20, 1997, 44.

3. *The New York Times,* November 28, 1998.

4. S. Davis, "Space Jam and Family Values in the Entertainment City," paper presented at American Studies Annual Meeting, Washington, D.C., 1997.

5. J. Sterngold, "Editor of *Los Angeles Times* Quits Amid Shake-up," *The New York Times,* October 10, 1997, C-5.

6. "Socialist International," *Wall Street Journal,* December 17, 1997, A-22.

7. Suein L. Hwang, "How Philip Morris Got Turkey Hooked on American Tobacco," *Wall Street Journal,* September 11, 1998, 1.

8. Stacy Kravetz, "San Diego May Flush Now, Drink Later," *Wall Street Journal,* September 9, 1998, B-1.

CHAPTER FOUR

COMMUNICATION THEORISTS OF EMPIRE

I n college before World War II, I studied economics. It seemed like a realistic choice, given the millions of unemployed who were looking for work in those years. Not that I had much confidence that I would get a job, but economics, I reasoned, gave me a better shot at employment than a degree in the humanities. There was one other attraction to the field in those days—its subject matter. The problems of mass unemployment, a stalled economy, the role of the state in overcoming the crisis, were addressed by economists. This was stimulating stuff.

By the time the war was over, this had begun to change. The Depression had been overcome by massive injections of military expenditures. The postwar reconstruction boom was underway. The leaders of the big corporations had begun to reassert their authority, which had lapsed during the prolonged crisis. The economists dutifully followed the new centers of power. Postwar economics lost its interest for me, and I had an opportunity to move into a new field—communication—in the mid-1960s.

The shift was a happy one, but it brought me face to face with a familiar problem. Although a new area of study, communication no less than economics was already a discipline captured by big money and powerful interests. Still, it was a challenge to explore how this new sphere of knowledge was being driven by both old and new forces in the constantly changing, but enduring, system of profit making.

Some puzzling questions immediately came to the fore. The overriding one was, How did thinking that benefited the few gain the acceptance of the many? And what, for instance, did the country's intellectual leadership have to say about the power complex's extraordinary postwar march into world markets; or about much of the world's efforts to redistribute material and symbolic resources more evenly?

Obviously, there was no uniform response to these issues, but in the governing opinion, shared and shaped by the intellectual class—academic, government, and business—the support for the United States' international policy was solid, and especially evident in communication studies and research. Here, prevailing views not only defended U.S.-drafted programs of control and domination but also claimed that they were based on scientific principles.

Though economic, military, and pop cultural power have been the central pillars of American superpower over the last fifty years, the contribution of theory and research to this dominance, difficult as it is to measure, should not be slighted. It has armed U.S. practitioners with operative guidelines for their tasks, and, perhaps more consequentially, it has set the definitions for thinking about these matters in every place touched by American power. Especially in the ex-colonial regions, leaders and policy makers have been provided with principles on how to organize their societies that have come out of U.S. sources serving imperial policy.

The origins of cultural domination have long been been familiar. Marx wrote about it 150 years ago. In class-divided societies, efforts to explain social or physical phenomena will be heavily influenced by the perspectives and inclinations of the dominating stratum. J. D. Bernal put it this way: "The existence of class-divided societies does not affect only the material consequences of knowledge, it cuts deep into the root of ideas. The literate and cultured are the ruling class, and the basic ideas that find expression in literature and science are inevitably tinged with ruling-class preconceptions and self-jus-tifications."[1]

These basic ideas are themselves shaped by the social circumstances of their times. Ever since 1945, this has meant that American power has been the preeminent social circumstance of the era, and the extension of that power has been the singular goal of the power complex. As past experiences elsewhere led us to expect, seizing and holding world advantage has absorbed the attention of the country's intellectual leadership.

This way of looking at things does not mean that alternative explanations, in any period, are absent. What it generally signifies is that the strongest encouragement—financial support, economic position, and social esteem—invariably will be given to those theorists and researchers who provide findings that are at least comforting, and generally helpful, to the dominant order. No less important, these findings will obtain the widest circulation and attention from the reviews and publicity that are also at the disposal of the dominating power.

The last half-century of communication research and theorizing—undertaken in the United States—richly confirms these theses. At the end of World War II, the United States was the world's most powerful economy, economically energized by the conflict, politically secure, and culturally poised to capture the international symbolic sphere. Even at that time, it was a corporate-organized and highly concentrated system.

The strategic interests of this system were twofold. One was to deny the leftist mass movements in Western Europe, and elsewhere, their strong claim to move their societies in new, noncapitalist directions. The other vital goal was to extend U.S. economic and social influence over the newly independent and other Third World nations, while at the same time ensuring their envelopment in the world capitalist system.

As mentioned, a variety of means were employed to achieve these ends, including economic bribery, presented as "aid"—the essence of the Marshall Plan—and denial of "aid" if a state proved recalcitrant to American demands; the option of military intervention; and finally, massive persuasion, utilizing the new communication technologies in the hands of the state and commercial (pop cultural) sectors.

In implementing, justifying, and explaining theoretically these aggressive policies and actions, a new field of inquiry—

communication research—was born. Actually, communication research dates to the pre–World War II years, when it developed mostly as market research for the big consumer goods producers and the broadcasting industry that carried their sponsorship. Most of these early studies sought to identify the effectiveness of sales messages.

Yet it was only after the war that the field of communication research really blossomed. And no wonder! It was organically tied to the power centers of the age—military, corporate, and state, the force fields vigorously pursuing their designs of U.S. global ascendancy. No less important, the structural changes in the economy, then underway, made information and persuasion steadily more essential in the operation of a technologically advancing capitalist system, in the beginning at home and later on as underpinning for the global market economy.

As one historian recently put it:

As the political climate shifted in the late 1940s from the war against fascism to the crusade against communism, the basic concepts of communication research could be, and were, easily redeployed. How communication might build loyalty at home and stable, new, non-communist nations around the globe became critically important to the field. It was, in large part, the new, Cold War use of these concepts that made the field of communication research take off. By the mid-1950s, it was a richly funded area of inquiry....[2]

The absorption of the new sphere of communication into an instrument of class domination is not a unique example of systemic cooptation of a field of knowledge. Robert Heilbroner, in a work with William Milberg, for example, notes that "our discipline [economics]… is intrinsically embedded in capitalism and to some degree thereby becomes its self-justifying voice, even when it is quite oblivious of serving that purpose."[3] But the situation in communication research is unique in at least one respect. Its takeover was observable from its inception, the subordination of its practitioners glaringly overt. The aims it served were obvious. In other social and physical areas of knowledge, the influence of dominating class power may be more veiled, sometimes nearly invisible to casual observation.

The specific means employed to make communication research an adjunct of U.S. power have been masterfully documented by Christopher Simpson.[4] He recounts how the "founding fathers" of the new discipline were recruited to work for the Pentagon, the intelligence services, and the foreign policy establishment.

The connection and utility of communication research to American postwar expansive capitalism is both unmeasurable and measureless. The first communication contribution of critical importance to the early expansion was the creation of a hysterical atmosphere at home, quickly transported abroad, that enabled U.S. geopolitical designs to proceed with near total popular acceptance. This was achieved with the launching of a long-lasting and pervasive anticommunist crusade. The central argument justifying anticommunism and the overwhelming fear it generated was that the world was threatened by Soviet military aggression. This was nonsensical on the face of it—the Russians had just lost more than 20,000,000 people and were economically devastated—yet the orchestration of the powerful media system and the entire culture to this end made the threat credible and frightening.

Anticommunist rhetoric served to sanction and gloss socially destructive U.S. policies and actions over a fifty-year period. Communication scholarship and scholars actively participated in the creation and maintenance of this doctrine of falsification. Wilbur Schramm, for example, who became the leading figure in U.S. communication research, was a dedicated worker in the construction of the anticommunism climate. As early as 1950, in the first months of the Korean War, Schramm went to Korea under the auspices of the U.S. Air Force to survey Koreans who had been in Seoul during the brief Communist occupation.

Ignoring the complicated background of the Korean War—which one American historian viewed more as a civil war—Schramm and John W. Riley, Jr., published *The Reds Take a City: The Communist Occupation of Seoul*, a book whose propagandistic intent was set forth in its introduction, written by Frederick W. Williams: "As the authors of this book point out, the model of the Communist blueprint for Seoul was Pyongyang, Prague, Bucharest, Moscow. Here, then, is the lesson of Communist intentions, intentions which are being consistently planned for execution in every home—in city and on farm—around the world. In your home, too!"[5] Riley and Schramm's conclusion is no less emotional and demagogic:

"[The study] affirms our observation that the Communist system promises much to many but in fact delivers its rewards to only a few.... The free people of the world may take heart... [but] how many more such accounts must be written?"[6]

This was a foretaste of what was to come from communication researchers in the years to follow. Another project, in 1953, was a recipe-for-propaganda book produced under the direction of Schramm for the instruction of the U.S. Information Agency (USIA). Let it be recalled that this was an intense period of the Cold War in which the USIA was globally engaged in disseminating Washington's interpretations of American worldwide interventionism.

Suggestive of the atmosphere of that era, the study was classified for twenty years. When it was finally published commercially, in 1976, author Leo Bogart explained that the book's reappearance might help to restore the anticommunist perspective of the pre-Vietnam period. This, of course, required the expunging of the Vietnam experience, for as Bogart wrote, "A generation of intellectuals—including historians—were conditioned during the Vietnam War to question and oppose American foreign policy and to assume that its Communist opponents were the protagonists of oppressed people longing for redress of long-standing grievances." Additional academic contributions to the work of the USIA were also noted: "with the advice of Paul Lazarsfeld and his associates at Columbia University, the Voice of America in New York had built up an impressive research staff of 150, headed by the sociologist Leo

Lowenthal and including Ralph White, M. Fiske, Joseph T. Klapper and Harold Mendelsohn."[7]

Whatever the book's success in making its 1953 anticommunist premises more credible, it offers additional evidence of the unstinting cooperation communication scholarship supplied to postwar American imperial power. Another example is a book published by Schramm in 1957, *Responsibility in Mass Communication*, which, as Kenneth Cmiel writes, "reeks of Cold War apologetics."[8]

PROVIDING THE THEORETICAL UNDERPINNING

Alongside communication scholarship's ready service to the state machine that was organizing the world economy along lines agreeable to dominant economic interests in the United States was another, perhaps more important contribution; the new discipline supplied the theoretical models that underpinned vital segments of postwar American foreign policy. Exemplary here is the work of Daniel Lerner, who was, in British sociologist Jeremy Tunstall's view, the intellectual leader of a key group of American communication scholars, including Schramm and Ithiel DeSola Pool.[9]

Lerner was among the first to grasp, and to articulate, the geopolitical strategy of securing the ex-colonial world for Western-structured "development." In this, he helped found the new field of development communication, which incorporated this strategy in its underlying assumptions and practices.

In the many variants of developmental theory, communication played a key role, most importantly to instill the modernization idea in what the scholars regarded as hitherto passive
peoples. The media were supposed to be the catalytic force. Here
again, Cmiel writes: "By the mid-1950s... communication
research became a central pillar in what came to be known as
'modernization theory' and a part of the Cold War offensive
against communism. Mass communication was now seen as
critical to building loyalty to the modern nation-state and as a
theme of dozens of 1950s studies, including Lerner's very
influential work."[10]

Lerner understood that it was the "emergence of the Third
World" that constituted the grand prize at stake—as well as
being a determining factor in the long-term viability of the
world market system. He put the challenge to American postwar expansionist policy this way:

> The long era of imperialism (subordination) is recently
> ended; the campaign for international development
> (equalization) has just begun. In the new process, inter-
> national communication operates in behalf of different
> policy purposes under different socioeconomic condi-
> tions by different psychopolitical means. Indeed, in the
> transition from imperialism to international develop-
> ment, there has been a fundamental change in the role
> of communication. Under the new conditions of global-
> ism, it has largely replaced the coercive means by which

colonial territories were seized and held.... *The persua-sive transmission of enlightenment is the modern paradigm of international communication.*" (emphasis mine)[11]

Here indeed is the formula of late twentieth-century capital-ism that has been so effectively applied by U.S. policy makers and their international followers. Lerner's special talent rested in his recognition of the key role communication might (and did) play in the creation of the global market economy, with the United States at the center of the system. In Lerner's prescription, there is a "transition from coercion to communication." Here, Lerner embraced the Truman "Point Four" position that imperi-alism was dead and cooperation now characterized U.S.–poor country relationships.

Actually, coercion has by no means been absent in recent decades, and Lerner's formulation is applicable only if the ex-colonial area/nation has settled for a market economy and allowed itself to be absorbed in the dominant world business order. Those new or old states that have insisted on some mea-sure of autonomy in the social character and operation of their economies have faced unrelenting combinations of economic and military force.

The dozens of direct interventions, the organization of mili-tary coups, and the economic blockades imposed by Washington over the last forty years constitute a huge database of aggression. At the same time, the utilization of international communica-tion—once a region has been "stabilized"—has provided an essential ingredient for making the operational routines of the world commercial economy effective.

The ratios that American communication specialists calculated to indicate developmental levels—so many movie seats, newspapers, radio sets, and so on per capita—however trivial, did in fact, though certainly not intentionally, measure one important condition. They revealed how far a country had been propelled into the global market system and, relatedly, how deeply it had been penetrated by U.S. media products and services and outlooks. The ratios were a measure of the extent to which "the persuasive transmission of enlightenment" had occurred.

BRIEF PERIOD OF CHALLENGE TO THE DOMINANT PARADIGM (1960s–1970s)

A mini-crisis of sorts was experienced by communication scholarship—as in most other scientific fields—in the late 1960s and throughout most of the 1970s. It developed as a reaction to the general crisis affecting U.S. power. The civil rights upsurge, the emergence of the women's movement, and opposition to the bloody, imperialist war in Vietnam, for a brief moment shook Washington's imperial course. These movements encouraged and provided a receptive atmosphere for the work of a small number of researchers who had begun to question both the domestic and international foundations of the dominant communication paradigm. This critical work largely, though not exclusively, identified with the claims of the disadvantaged majority of states, as well as with domestically voiceless groups, for a new, international information order. It detailed how unilateral and top-down was the flow of information, inside and between nations. It sought to reduce the Western monopoly on information flows; to expand the number of voices in the media arena; and to lessen the pervasive commercialism that enveloped the cultural climate in all areas subject to Western, mostly United States, media product.

For about a decade, the hegemony of establishment communication theory and scholarship was on the defensive, and cultural imperialism, when not ignored or ridiculed by prevailing communication scholarship as well as the industrial media practitioners, emerged for a moment as a discussable concept. It was in this fleeting period that one of the long-standing proponents of orthodoxy, Everett Rogers, published an essay entitled "Communication and Development: The Passing of the Dominant Paradigm," which claimed that the theoretical principles underlying U.S. communication development policy had been deficient and were no longer serviceable.[12]

Rogers's appraisal of the doctrine's failings may have been correct, but his view that it was no longer credible was mistaken. American domination in theory and practice reasserted itself by the end of the 1970s. Viewed in historical context, Ronald Reagan's election as president of the United States in 1980 was not a random political development; it signaled an offensive, more ferocious than ever, by American capitalism, to extend world market share, destroy socialism, and intensify the exploitation of working people. Sadly, the field of communication scholarship quickly got in step with the latest guardians of systemic power.

THE NEW, AND IMPROVED, DOMINANT PARADIGM

To fully appreciate the curious world of communication scholarship over the years since Rogers's acknowledgment of its earlier deficiencies, it is helpful to pause briefly over the publicly recorded developments in the private cultural industries of this period.

The last fifteen years in the United States, and in Western Europe have witnessed an unprecedented increase in the concentration of ownership and control in the communication sector. Publishing, radio, TV, film, recording, and telecommunications have been assembled into huge conglomerate enterprises, representing hitherto unimaginable concentrated cultural power. Corporations such as Time Warner, Disney-Capital Cities-ABC, Murdoch's News Corporation, Viacom-CBS, Bertelsman, and half a dozen other telecommunications and computer software giants now preside over the global symbolic environment.

Preceding and facilitating this massive transformation in the character of private cultural production and dissemination have been the twin movements of deregulation and privatization. After being initiated in the U.K. (Margaret Thatcher) and the United States (circa the Reagan era), these policies have been carried out in one country after another, wherever the transnational corporate order prevails. In fact, this means, with a couple of minor exceptions, everywhere.

These two movements, selling off public sector enterprises to private capital and reducing, when not eliminating, social accountability of corporate enterprise, have had an especially baleful impact on the product of the communication industries. In the United States, they have enabled an almost unlimited pyramidization of TV, film, radio, and publishing properties into what were already powerful corporate hands. They have also largely stripped away what modest public oversight existed over the cultural industries: TV, radio, and the press, in particular.[13] Experiences in Europe, West and East, when not identical, are similar, taking national specificities into account.

All of this has led to the existing situation wherein a good part of the world's cultural production is manufactured and distributed by corporate entities. Independents and small-scale private producers remain, but they exist on the margins or as feeder tributaries to the big companies.

This is the communication-cultural context that exists, whether it is recognized or not by researchers in the field. Given this condition, one might imagine that the time is propitious for studies of corporate cultural power, such as comparative studies, of how national systems of broadcasting and telecommunications have been privatized; an examination of techniques of subduing, misleading, or pacifying message receivers; accounts and analyses of media subservience to, or collaboration with corporate and political power; the implications of excessive corporate power for freedom of the press, if not the very principle of a free press; critiquing the introduction of new information technologies; and assessing what corporate "speech" means for individual speech. Numerous other questions come to mind that, if examined, could illuminate the communication condition in a time of far-reaching monopoly.

Some of these studies may in fact already have been undertaken.[14] But the attention of most scholarship has been directed elsewhere. It has centered on *audience* research: the receivers, not the producers, of the symbolic material. Oliver Boyd-Barrett, writing in 1995, opines, "If obliged to define a single distinguishing feature of media study over the past 15 years, many scholars would focus on new approaches to audience or 'reception' analysis."[15] James Curran described this development, nonpejoratively, as "revisionist" theory.[16] This turnabout bears a striking resemblance to what occurred half a century earlier. In the late 1930s, "effects research" served to divert attention from the powerful role of persuasion and who were the persuaders.[17]

Actually, audience research could be a fruitful area to study, *if* informed by the context of the current period of media colossi. If it were motivated by a desire to do battle with the controlling corporate cultural forces of the day, some very interesting work could be expected. Perhaps there is such work underway, but unfortunately the bulk of the research, consciously or not, has a different objective. It serves to *deny* the influence of the prevailing corporate cultural infrastructure, at the same time insisting that individuals (audiences) are actively and successfully engaged in resisting, *subjectively*, the messages and images of the Disneys, Time Warners, and Viacoms.

This emphasis on audience resistance, and an accompanying indifference to, if not denial of, corporate symbolic domination, contributes—whatever the researchers engaged may think or claim—to a grotesque distortion of reality. It weakens, actually undermines, any effort to tangibly resist corporate cultural domination. Boyd-Barrett notes noncommittally, "Revisionism [audience research] undermines the force of the radical critique of mass communication in that it serves the interests of the powerful and contributes to the social reproduction of inequality."[18]

Graham Murdock is less distanced. He writes, "The stark vertical structures of inequality have been bulldozed off this [revisionist theory] map and the economic and political dynamics that have built them have slid from view.... Class has become a category that dare not speak its name."[19]

The impact of revisionist theory is not limited to the United States and the U.K. Active audience proponents deny the influence, sometimes even the existence, of global cultural power. The audiences in countries receiving the monopoly cultural flows are claimed by revisionist theorists to be unaffected because each audience makes its own interpretations of the products entering its senses. In effect, if the active audience theorists have it right, the efforts of 130 or so countries in the late 1960s and early 1970s to change their informational environments because they were dominated by external, monopoly forces were misplaced. In revisionist theory, cultural imperialism, like inequality and class, "slides from view." So, for example,

Elihu Katz and Tamar Liebes began their study *The Export of Meaning*, with this sentence: "Theorists of cultural imperialism assume that hegemony is prepackaged in Los Angeles, shipped out to the global village, and unwrapped in innocent minds."[20]

This caricature of cultural domination is an easy construction for these writers to demolish, but the reality is more substantial. The material world of privileged economic interests and class power does not disappear. In fact, it asserts itself regularly in pursuit of its well understood needs. How paradoxical that representatives of power have no difficulty in referring to domination, while so many communication researchers seem unable to utter the word!

Popular hopes in many countries have been frustrated. Social policies that might have been beneficial to the majority have been turned aside. Decisions taken under U.S. influence have launched arms races that have wasted huge amount of resources and money. International political institutions have been weakened, subverted, or circumvented, largely under U.S. pressure. The global economy has been handed over to a few thousand giant transnational corporations, not all, but many, American-owned.

To achieve these perverse goals, the ideas and prescriptions of the country's governing class, contributed by intelligence-agency-financed think tanks, grant-receiving academics in the elite schools, and foundation-sponsored studies, have been vital. Strategies conceived at MIT, for example, provided the economic developmental policies that were imposed on much of the ex-colonial world. That these policies bore the mark of their ultimate corporate parentage was rarely acknowledged. Instead, the impeccable intellectual credentials of the formulators burnished the work. Funding connections to the defense, intelligence, and corporate complex emerged, if at all, long after the studies and programs had had their frequently devastating impact.

Influencing other cultures' leaders, and prospective leaders, has become a big and busy industry in the United States. In the late 1990s nearly half a million foreign students enrolled annually in American colleges and universities. Foreign editors, publishers, and media people were taken for frequent, expense-paid junkets to U.S. installations. The most prestigious U.S. universities have established centers—like corporate branch plants—across Europe to enroll that part of the population well-off enough to afford the high tuition costs. European and other executives are trained in U.S. business schools. In the less visible infrastructure of control, databases compiled in the United States, whose definitions and categories are embedded in the data, comprise the bulk of information now accessible worldwide.

What began as a highly focused effort, enlisting American intellectuals to create programs that would push people and countries in directions favorable to American power, has grown into a comprehensive institutional effort, densely intersecting with systemic interests at the global level. Theory and research are no less affected and guided today than they were in the 1940s and 1950s, when Cold War objectives were primary. At this time, there is no global adversary to American power, though this may change; what stimulates and supports U.S. research and theory today are market forces. There is scant demand for intellectual work that questions current institutional relationships. Where would it come from? From the corporate monoliths that oversee the social landscape? Grant givers, without being censorious, can defend their generally noncontroversial decisions as in keeping with prevailing status quo sentiments. Fifty years ago, the state directed its research monies to the military/defense intellectuals. Today, in the age of transnational business, funds are channeled into one or another form of marketing.

This poses a still unresolved and transcendent question. Will those informed in communication theory and research continue to serve systemic power as so many of them have dutifully done over the last half century? Or will they apply their capabilities and talent toward critical assessment of the institutional structures now in place? Though a field's integrity, no less than the nation's well-being, is at stake, we cannot be confident of the answer.

NOTES

1. J. D. Bernal, *Science In History* (London: Watts & Co., 1954), 886.

2. Kenneth Cmiel, "On Cynicism, Evil, and the Discovery of Communication in the 1940s," *Journal of Communication* 46, no. 3 (Summer 1996): 95.

3. Robert Heilbroner and William Milberg, *The Crisis of Vision in Modern Economic Thought* (Cambridge: Cambridge University Press, 1995), 127.

4. Christopher Simpson, *Science of Coercion: Communication Research and Psycho-*

logical Warfare, 1945-1960 (New York: Oxford University Press, 1996).

5. W. Schramm and John W. Riley, Jr., *The Reds Take a City: The Communist Occupation of Seoul* (New Brunswick, N.J.: Rutgers University Press, 1951), v–vii.

6. Ibid., 206.

7. Leo Bogart, *Premises for Propaganda: The United States Information Agency's Operating Assumptions in the Cold War* (New York: Free Press-Macmillan, 1976), ix.

8. Cmiel, "On Cynicism," 95.

9. Jeremy Tunstall, *The Media Are American* (New York: Columbia University Press, 1977), 208.

10. Cmiel, "On Cynicism," 96.

11. Daniel Lerner, "Managing Communication for Modernization: The Development Construct," in *Politics, Personality and Social Science in the Twentieth Century: Essays in Honor of Harold D. Lasswell,* ed. Arnold A. Rogow (Chicago: University of Chicago Press, 1969), 182.

12. In *Communication Research* 3, no. 2 (April 1976): 213–240.

13. Herbert I. Schiller, "The United States," in *Media Ownership and Control* (London: International Institute of Communication, 1996), 249–260.

14. The most biting commentaries about the information environment in the late 1990s have come, of all places, from Hollywood films. *Weapons of Mass Distraction, Wag the Dog,* and *The Truman Show* offer humorous and pointed criticism of the controlled image and message.

15. Oliver Boyd-Barrett, "Approaches to New Audience Research," in *Approaches to Media,* ed. Oliver Boyd-Barrett and Chris Newbold, (London: Arnold, 1995), 498.

16. James Curran, "The New Revisionism in Mass Communication Research: A Reappraisal," in Boyd-Barrett and Newbold, *Approaches to Media,* 505–511.

17. Cmiel, "On Cynicism," 92–93. See also Dan Schiller, *Theorizing Communication* (New York: Oxford University Press, 1997).

18. Boyd-Barrett, "Approaches to New Audience Research," 500.

19. Graham Murdock, "Across the Great Divide: Cultural Analysis and the Condition of Democracy," *Critical Studies in Mass Communication* 12, no. 1 (March 1995): 91.

20. Tamar Liebes and Elihu Katz, *The Export of Meaning: Cross Cultural Readings of Dallas* (New York: Oxford University Press, 1990), v.

CHAPTER FIVE

CORPORATIZING
COMMUNICATION
AND CULTURE

The support of Numero Uno's general population for its postwar imperial policy, with the exception of the Vietnam War, has been steadfast, though there is reason enough to imagine a different response. This is so because there are deep structural faults in the superpower edifice that make it a potentially unstable order. The distribution of wealth and power in the United States, for example, is increasingly unequal. Yet it has been keeping this system intact, domestically and internationally, that has motivated the many U.S.-inspired coups, military interventions, economic sanctions and blockades, and financial maneuvers in the last several decades.

So living in the number one society does not confer well-being and authority on every resident. Far from it! Despite the enormous wealth present in the United States, and its supplementation with tributary flows from the rest of the world, individual shares are wildly uneven. Most of the benefits accrue to a relatively small stratum at the top of the social pyramid, though there is a considerable runoff to the middle layers. Living in the number one society, therefore, is a very different experience for the corporate elite and its support groups than it is for the rest of the crowd. Inequality and powerlessness have not disappeared in the digital era. Electronics, much as it is touted as the basis for a new egalitarianism, may be putting heavier stresses on the existing faults.

The socioeconomic system that has dominated the world for the last 500 years, and which has existed in the United States since its founding, is capitalism. Capitalism cannot be reduced to one or a few features, but it does possess one relationship, central to its existence and operation, that constitutes the essence of inequality and ineradicable instability: the wage labor-capital connection that dwells at the heart of the system.

This is so because wage labor has to be available to the owners of capital if production is to be undertaken. Wage labor's identifying feature is its utter dependence on a wage for survival. Historically, wage labor has been torn from its earlier connection to an agricultural existence, which provided at least a minimum subsistence. When losing this subsistence base, "free" workers (actually, individuals stripped of their means of survival) face capital in their search for a livelihood. How much more unequal can a relationship be?

For this reason, inequality in a capitalist economy is not a minor deformation excisable by a fortuitous humane leader or the emergence of some new miracle technology, but an inseparable and basic feature of the social order. It may be reduced, but only up to a point. Only a radical transformation of society can begin to eliminate inequality.

Over the centuries some of this utter dependence has been

lessened, from time to time, by meliorative social movements and political action. Social policy that has striven to reduce inequality is itself entirely dependent on the strength or absence of mass social movements and political organizations. In the last century, social efforts toward the reduction of inequality have succeeded for a time to a point of seriously weakening the dependence of wage earners on capital. The social benefits of the (very partial) welfare state, only a twentieth century development, did begin to alter some of the terms of the structured inequality of the wage contract, yet there was nothing permanent about this. In fact, it began to change after World War II, accompanying the phenomenal increase in the strength of U.S. capitalism. Accelerating in the last twenty-five years, the drive to reverse the socially meliorative policies established earlier in the century now constitutes the political agenda of most of the Western world and the United States in particular.

Deregulation has been one of the most far-reaching goals of the new agenda, spurring the abandonment of social oversight while fostering a spectacular concentration of private assets. Closely related, the last quarter of this century also has seen a ferocious attack by capital on the public social sphere, leading either to its drastic curtailment or, in some instances, to its elimination. Federal regulatory agencies mandated to oversee vital functions of the economy—the production and quality of food, the safety of drugs, the responsibilities of commercial broadcasters, the security of the financial system, and so on—have had their oversight capabilities sharply scaled back. Staff appointments to these agencies often have been hostile to their mandated responsibilities.

In this same period, the resources of private companies heretofore subject to monitoring have grown enormously. In addition to robust internal growth, a vast merger movement has swept over the nation's productive base, transforming what were already large corporations into giant enterprises. A summary of the extent of this recent pyramiding of assets and resources notes:

> Not since a wave of industrial takeovers created the great oil, steel and auto companies at the beginning of the century has corporate America been reshaped by a sweep of merger activity as broad as the the one taking place today.... Last year [1997] alone, a record $1 trillion in mergers took place involving American companies, a pace almost unrivalled in business history.... In 1997, there were 156 mergers of $1 billion or more involving American companies.... In the last five years, there have been 2,492 mergers worth more than $200 billion among commercial banks; 1,435 deals worth $162 billion in radio and television....

The report concluded, "So far, little concern has been expressed in Washington."[1]

This, in brief, represents a snapshot of a rampaging capitalism, literally out of control. The inequality inherent in the wage labor/capital relationship is made more overwhelming by this surge in capital's growth. It is deepened and extended further by the fierce antilabor policies initiated in the 1980s in the Reagan years. Against a state complicit with capital's interests, a terribly weakened organized labor movement has little leverage on industrial, let alone social policy.

The inequality does not end with powerful postindustrial capital enjoying the state's benevolence; the growing media/cultural combines that manufacture and circulate the nation's symbolic environment make their substantial contribution as well. The concentration in the industrial/financial sectors of the economy is matched in the nation's cultural industries and institutions. In the press, the daily news, such as it is—are disseminated by a tiny number of chains that own papers in scores of cities. The local, pluralistic press has long vanished, and the great majority of communities, including most of the biggest cities, are now one-newspaper locales.

Television—the supreme communicator—along with publishing and retail bookselling, has been swept up by a handful of media combines. "Fewer than ten colossal vertically integrated media conglomerates," Robert McChesney reports, "now dominate U.S. media."[2] Each of the four major TV networks (ABC, NBC, CBS, Fox) is owned by a supercorporation —Disney, General Electric, Viacom, and Murdoch's News Corporation. Cable television, once seen as the alternative, is in the hands of fewer than half a dozen giant firms.

Powerful and concentrated as these entities are, they are all heavily dependent on the advertising expenditures of the now-global goods and services producers; the car companies, the consumer goods titans, the drug and pharmaceutical firms. The revenues of TV come exclusively from these sponsors. For press and magazines, reliance on advertising reaches well beyond 50 percent and is often as high as 70 percent of revenues.

This vital connection between media and the economy's industrial core is a dominant feature of late-twentieth-century capitalism. TV provides the most spectacular means for transforming the audience into consumers. To obtain that audience is the holy grail of TV producers. When Dan Rather, the anchor of CBS News, along with other national anchors, was pulled out of Havana, where he was covering the Pope's visit, the reason was a juicier story—the president's latest sexual episode. Rather was quoted as saying, "I just didn't think it was practical to say no." *New York Times* TV columnist Walter Goodman put it this way: "The three masters of the media were not permitted by *their* masters to follow their better angels; our men in Havana had to follow that woman. 'It's about circulation and ratings,' Mr. Rather lamented. 'It's about competitive pressures.'"[3]

And herein lies the grand dilemma facing those who would challenge the many derelictions of the number one society. Any serious effort to change the social order collides head-on with the fundamental interests of the corporate industrial system. And that system has at its disposal the informational apparatus and the cultural institutions that influence, if not determine, social thinking.

This explains why informational and cultural power have

become key factors in governance. How these are deployed is no less decisive for social control than are the army and the police.

In recent years, the power of capital has grown, while the public's strength has weakened. This is observable in everyday economic measures. The return to property explodes while labor's share in the social product contracts. In the twenty-five years that have seen the transformation of U.S. business from national to global actor, profits are up and living standards of the general population are either stagnant or in decline, though a brief reversal has been apparent in the last couple of years of the current boom. Most of the material measures of equality have declined in the last quarter of a century. Income distribution, perhaps the most important gauge, has grown increasingly lopsided. It is to be expected that in a period in which capital's relative and absolute strength is at its peak, it has the power to compel a more favorable division of the social product to itself—and so it has gone and continues to go.

NONMATERIAL POWER

More portentous still, similar trends are observable in the non-material fields of power. The output and control of the economy's cultural and intellectual product have also, largely and increasingly, become the proprietary holdings of Numero Uno's directing elite.

Nonmaterial inequality arises from the terms under which

the nation's symbolic production is created and distributed. If the producers are giant, profit-seeking private enterprises, the distribution of symbolic goods will be no less unequal than the distribution of income. The conditions of symbolic goods production will also affect their quality, their comprehensiveness, and the channels of their distribution.

Vital questions of social existence are involved. Most consequential: how can a democratic discourse exist in a corporate-owned informational system? Who, for example, possesses freedom of speech in such a society? And who sets the direction of scientific and technological discovery, and organizes the ends to which these discoveries are put? Finally, where has all the public space gone? Is it still possible to schmooze in a non-corporate environment?

These are but a few of the dimensions that constitute the less tangible side of life. Recent years point to deepening inequality in the nonmaterial sphere of American existence.

SOURCES OF DECLINING NONMATERIAL LIVING STANDARDS: Deregulation and its Costs

Deregulation and privatization have been two of the insistent demands of capital in the post–World War II decades. Deregulation has been, above all else, a means of reducing corporate business's accountability to the public. It does this by seeking to eliminate, or at least greatly reduce, social monitoring of corporate activity. Privatization eliminates sites of public

(state) economic activity and transfers them to corporate ownership. Together, deregulation and privatization signal the
destruction of the not-for-profit sector of economic and social
activity and the shrinking of the arena of public involvement.
Consequently they produce an all-embracing condition of
commercialism and commodity relationships.

What this means is that commercial criteria and practices
permeate the social order. All transactions are governed by
market rules, the foremost of which is the criterion of the ability to pay. Once everything is for sale and ability to pay for a
purchase is the central determining factor, inequality is guaranteed; who can pay becomes the one and only standard, and
exclusion by inability to pay an invisible side effect. This criterion also signifies the thinning of the symbolic output, reduced
by the market's indifference to considerations that are not
profit producing. With the hardening of the for-profit-only
standard, the impoverishment of nonmaterial life deepens in
the core of the world system. Evidence of this is not difficult to
find.

THE CORPORATE TAKEOVER OF THE CULTURE

School activities, once outside the realm of direct moneymaking,
are now incorporated into the marketing system. Commercial
TV, *designed* for the classroom, is currently broadcast in their
classrooms to millions of school children, who view commercials
as part of their curriculum. The physical sites of the schools are
being transformed into selling spaces, as Pepsi-Cola, Coca-Cola,

running shoe companies, and computer software distributors, fiercely compete for deals with financially strapped school administrators and coaches.

Organized sports reveal still more sharply the corporatization of the game and the growth of a structured inequality imposed on the fans (audiences). Baseball franchises, for example, once the prestige possessions of wealthy individuals, increasingly are properties of large corporations that use the game as fodder, programming if you will, for their major television and broadcasting holdings. Disney owns the Anaheim Angels in California. Ted Turner owns the Atlanta Braves, and most recently, Rupert Murdoch has acquired the Los Angeles Dodgers. One of the effects of this development is a growing disparity between the resources of the conglomerate-held team and the other franchises. The wealthy corporate owners buy the most expensive talent as a matter of course. The circle of winners is tightened. The losers, the majority, stumble along hoping for an unlikely windfall.

The fans too, are divided into elites and Joe Six-Packs. As soon as Murdoch bought the Los Angeles team, inequality took a giant leap forward. In Dodger Stadium, a new level of advertising was introduced, and luxury suites were built in the park: "Seventy-five to eighty suites [that] should lease for at least $200,000 each, the peak price in baseball."[4] The occupants of these fancy and pricey suites will be corporate executives and their customers, just as tickets in the championship games go first to the big moneymen, and the general public gets what's left over. Sportsmanship and sports in the corporate age require redefinition. Their primary feature has become inequality.

In recent years, journalism, not a newcomer to commercialism, has become awash in what is called market-driven journalism; otherwise put, this denotes the acknowledged primacy of commercial over editorial decision making. An ever-cozier relation of advertisers with editors, at first noted with alarm, has become routine. What this means for the quality of the information disseminated to the general public may be imagined.

And what is one to think of corporate museums? Yes, corporate museums. Individual companies are establishing accounts of their own history; e.g., "The World of Coca-Cola," "Hershey's Chocolate World," Motorola, Deere & Co., Goodyear, Toyota, Kellogg's (with its "Cereal City, USA"), Intel, and Microsoft have gone in for private installations detailing their growth and operations. "The corporate museum is taking off," according to the author of a guide of company-sponsored sites.[5]

The more museums the better, but if these corporate installations become the definitive narrative of the field, will their accounts represent the full experience of all the participants? Labor's role and experiences, for instance, and consumer attitudes to the company product—will they find room in the company's presentation?

In medicine and science, the profit-seeking goals of giant pharmaceutical, drug, and bioengineering companies prevail over social needs, and often over scientific accuracy. From this all-encompassing commercial atmosphere emerges a new con-

stellation of symbolic production. Ventures that promise profitability are supported. Those that cannot offer such prospects
are ignored. This becomes the fundamental calculus in determining scientific and social activity. A corporate-dominated
economy, lacking strong social direction and oversight, can be
expected to generate ideas, data, and products of interest and
value primarily to its paying constituents, leaving social needs
largely unattended. This condition now extends to information
generation in general.

The national government, historically the largest generator
of information in the country, finds its functions reduced at
the insistence of capital ("market forces"). Corporate information
production, now greatly expanded, remains for the most part
proprietary and therefore off-limits to public scrutiny. The
effect of this developing situation, yet to be fully experienced,
is a national community less and less likely to obtain the basic
information it requires to make effective policies on behalf of
the public.

In creative fields, the expanded influence of corporate
bottom-line calculation is ever more blatant and brazen. It
intrudes on filmmaking, television production, and theatrical
productions. In 1996, according to the Motion Picture Association of America, "the average cost of making and marketing a
movie rose to nearly $60 million." For intended blockbuster
films, the costs escalate to at least $100 million to make and
$20 million–30 million to market.[6] There are, to be sure, many
films made with much lower outlays, but for the most part
these gain at best a marginal share of the national audience.

When the average investment in a film reaches these astronomical levels, a whole set of market forces come into play. The content of the script, the choice of director and actors, the selection of marketing options, and the timing of the release all become critical commercial considerations, reviewed and decided by money managers, not filmmakers.

The films thus produced cannot avoid reflecting no-risk, status quo choices associated with the management and safeguarding of capital: with rare exceptions do films get made that ruffle feathers. What most of them do is to provide heavy doses of diversion to already distracted audiences. The absence of critical, oppositional, and truly imaginative content—as contrasted with technology-laden futurist scenarios—amounts to a denial of the potential of film and the disregard of human potential as well.

In the theater the situation is no less pernicious. Resisting all efforts over time to establish nationally supported theater ensembles, the profit imperative has transformed a great part of theatrical life, at least in New York City, the long-standing hub of the theater, into a site for the production, and exportation to the rest of the country, of multimillion-dollar musical extravaganzas. These are regarded as good investments by the moneymen because they are fabricated concoctions, congenial to the affluent suburbanites, out for a night of undemanding entertainment, to the large contingent of brokers and security analysts in Wall Street, and to the well-heeled foreign tourists who seek titillation in the big city. Once stamped with Broadway success and publicized nationally by platoons of media flacks and touts, these productions are sent on the road, filling theaters in dozens of cities across the country. In addition to being extremely profitable locally, they succeed in grabbing playing space—auditoria and halls—and audiences, and threatening the survival of bona fide theatrical companies.[7] New York City itself has had a big chunk of its historic entertainment center, Times Square, transformed into a display space for a few of the biggest U.S. cultural conglomerates, foremost of which is the Disney corporation.

What does this account of appropriation of cultural space by corporate giants have to do with the growing social and economic inequality that now characterizes the American social landscape, weakening the democratic fiber of the country? Simply this: How will voices that might express opposition to the deepening inequality and public-sector immiseration be heard? Through what channels can they express their challenges? Can they be expected to develop in schools engulfed by commercialism, many on their way toward privatization? Will organized sports, now tied tightly to sponsorship and corporate ownership, be a venue for the expression of fairness and community benefit? Will market-driven journalism provide public enlightenment?

Will medicine and science, hitched to the corporate patron, step in to call attention to the unraveling ecological scene, much less to the dangers of hastily marketed drugs? What about corporate museums? How much useful social knowledge will they reveal? Will $100 million films take up serious social issues? Will network TV, in the hands of four supercorporations, report reality or produce programming that explains it? And will Broadway musicals supply social meaning for their mostly affluent customers?

Yet these—our means of cultural expression—are the essential instruments with which Numero Uno could be called to account, and alternatives discussed. Lamentably, today they are used either to divert attention from underlying conditions or to trivialize or cosmeticize them. Such is the impasse, with its all too likely continuing impoverishment of nonmaterial life in the world's self-satisfied sole superpower.

CONCLUSION

On a global scale, the functions of most nation-states will erode further as their capabilities are transferred to global corporations and the workings of the global capital markets. The most important remaining task of national governments will be policing their restless populations. The atrophy of the democratic political system will continue, if not accelerate, undermined by its impotence to manage the global economic system while its constituents are the beneficiaries of torrents of TV commercials exhorting them to buy whatever is on offer.

It is possible that the new instrumentation will offer surprises that to some extent may negate these outcomes, but given the main custodians of the networks, this is unlikely. Social interventions too may push for some softening of these developments, but these are still to manifest themselves. Reluctantly, therefore, we must conclude that only one vision of the emerging electronic networked order is realistically sustainable at the present time. A human and socially based usage, for the time being at least, is a fantasy. The corporate interest prevails.

What we might envisage at some future date—however distant—is a publicly funded network in which the manifold creative, educational, and social welfare needs of all will take precedence over the balance sheet–determined commercial product, increasing exponentially as the current system comes into full operation.

But for the short term, the picture is not a pretty one.

NOTES

1. Leslie Wayne, "The Merger Movement," *The New York Times*, January 19, 1998, 1.

2. Robert McChesney, *Corporate Media and the Threat to Democracy* (New York: Seven Stories Press, 1997), 18.

3. Walter Goodman, "Melancholy Moments in TV's Coverage of a Scandal," *The New York Times*, February 3, 1998, B-2.

4. Richard Sanomir, "Warily, Baseball Prepares to Make Murdoch Owner of the Dodgers," *The New York Times*, March 8, 1998, 1.

5. Carl Quintanilla, "Planning a Vacation? Give Some Thought to Spam-town USA," *Wall Street Journal*, April 30, 1998, 1.

6. Bernard Weintraub, "Average Hollywood Film Now Costs $60 Million," *The New York Times*, March 5, 1997, B-8.

7. Edward Tothstein, "A Shifting American Landscape," *The New York Times*, December 6, 1998, B-1.

CHAPTER SIX

IN THE CORE OF POWER

T*he New York Times Magazine*, in a full issue devoted to "How the World Sees Us," provides an assessment of U.S. preeminence:

The crumbling of the Berlin Wall in 1989 marked the beginning of America's ascendancy to a new level of world domination. No traveler can miss the evidence abroad. In music, television and movies, America's influence is approaching what advertising people call "market saturation." The emblems of American mass culture have infiltrated the remotest outposts: the Coca-Cola logo is on street corners from Kazakhstan to Bora-Bora; CNN emanates from television sets in more than 200 countries; there are more 7-Eleven stores in Japan than in the United States. Our technology—computerized weapons systems, medical scanners, the Internet—sets the standard to which developing countries aspire.[1]

Yet how the world sees us may not be as revealing as how we see ourselves. How do those who reside in this globally preeminent territory understand their own and their country's situation? Is it, in fact, so obvious to everyone, as they go about their daily routines, that they are part of a dominating global order? When, if at all, do people in this ruling core society express indignation at, or resistance to, the burdens their order imposes on others—and frequently on themselves as well?

This awareness cannot be taken for granted; nor does it inevitably surface. Indeed, the far-reaching enterprise of being the global overlord requires not indignation but support, or at least acquiescence, from the people who inhabit its home territory, some 265 million of them.

Up to the present time, this has been achieved in a multi-faceted way, combining heavy indoctrination that begins in the cradle with a complex system of selection and/or omission of information that reinforces the enterprise's maintenance and growth. Along with intense, though often veiled, efforts of persuasion, and equally extensive exclusion of potential discordancies, there is a well-graded arsenal of coercions that begins with admonition and ends with incarceration. (More people are in prison, proportionally, in the United States than anywhere else on earth.)

Together, to date, these instruments of social control have been remarkably successful in producing, if not enthusiastic believers, at least general acceptance at home of the American control apparatus and its procedures for running the world. Justifying this endeavor are continual reminders by the governing class of how blessed everyone is, at home and abroad, by the present arrangements.

The refrain of America's greatness echoes throughout the land in the post–World War II years. One president after another, from Truman to Reagan to Clinton, tells us how wonderful we are. In 1997, for example, Hillary Clinton, not a president but married to one, quoting Alexander de Toqueville —a favorite source for political pontificators—modestly concludes that "America [is] the strongest and best nation in the history of the world."[2]

Not only at the present time, but apparently since Neanderthal days, the country is without peer. Another assessment, coming from the former managing director of Kissinger Associates, as strong a credential as any for credibility in governing ranks, is no less assertive: "The United States should not hesitate to promote its values," David Rothkopf writes, and, as previously mentioned, further asserts that America has historically proven herself to be "the best model for the future."[3]

This is the view, at the end of the twentieth century, that envelops American consciousness. How can anyone not recognize the bliss of living in the United States at this time? Yet many do not. Assertion, apparently, is not enough. More comprehensive methods of securing popular adherence, never absent in the past, are refined and calibrated for the millennium ahead.

DEFINITIONAL CONTROL

One of the most tested and effective means of keeping order in the ranks comes from *definitional control*: the ability to explain, and circulate, the governors' view of reality, local or global. This capability serves to bulwark, or at least minimize threats to, the prevailing social order. But this capability is not a loose football, waiting for someone to grab it. Its practice is dependent on a reliable national instructional system. Schools, entertainment, the media, and the political process are enlisted. The basis of definitional control, accordingly, is the informational infrastructure that produces meaning and (un)awareness.

When the infrastructure is in place and performing routinely, the exercise of definitional control is generally invisible, and almost always reflexive. It needs no prompting or instruction from the top of the social pyramid. It comes into play effortlessly and seemingly guilelessly. Throughout life, from infancy on, Americans, like all others, absorb the images and messages of the prevailing social order. These make up their frame of reference and perception. With few exceptions, it is this framework that insulates most people from ever imagining an alternative social reality.

Let us observe a recent application of frame of reference social control to an international event: the seizure by Tupac Amaru guerrillas of the Japanese embassy in Lima, Peru, in December 1996.

Some context is essential for understanding the process. U.S. foreign policy has long had as one of its central objectives the protection and well-being of American capital invested abroad, in plants or securities. This has necessitated over the years countless interventions, military and economic, and numberless coups against leaders perceived to be hostile to U.S. interests. As U.S. corporations are the central players in the global corporate economy, Washington is always on the alert for threats, real or imagined, to its main constituents— big business. At the same time, it must justify to the general public why troops are sent to this or that region, why loans are granted or withheld, why there is a revolving door through which so many foreign leaders are pushed.

From this perspective, the guerrilla siege in Lima, Peru, was, from Washington's vantage point, another more or less workaday episode that required a suitable frame of reference, in which the domestic, as well as overseas, public(s) would be able to appreciate what Washington claimed this dramatic event signified: nothing at all, except the criminal behavior of the hostage takers.

From the outset of the crisis, U.S. government leaders and spokespeople adopted the same explanation that the president of Peru, Fujimori, offered. He described the guerrillas as "terrorists" who had to be destroyed. With this definition of the situation, attention was easily diverted from the root causes of social unrest in Peru. Never mind also that in the bloody resolution of the affair, the guerrillas refrained from killing any of the hostages though they had ample means of doing so. The Peruvian military were not as generous, executing even those who tried to surrender.

After the event, a *New York Times* report quoted a local shopkeeper who said about the guerrilla leader, "He was not a terrorist. He was a revolutionary."[4]

But *revolutionary* is not an acceptable term to those who benefit from, and deny at the same time, the savage exploitativeness of the social system. Terrorists exist, to be sure; but the use of the term by the advantaged class is a means of disparaging and condemning those who strive to change rotten conditions of life for the many. In the Peruvian case, the terrorist label helped to relieve U.S. policy makers from the embarrassment of long-standing complicity with the ugly and coercive regime of Fujimori.

In the United States, the issue of terrorism, at home and abroad, has become a high governmental concern, and a justification for enormous military and police expenditures. And well it might be.

Definitional control is necessary for all governing classes, but it is extraordinarily important for the world's Numero Uno. It is no surprise—indeed, it is to be expected—that resistance to oppressive conditions will erupt from time to time in one coerced province or another. How are these outbreaks—which may be bloody and violent—to be explained to the U.S. population, and to other potentially resistant forces throughout the world? Consider how often the terrorist label is employed. In the 1990s, the Irish, the Iranians, the Libyans, the Palestinians, the Kurds, and numerous others have been so branded. In Colombia, where insurgent forces have been fighting for years to change an oppressive social order, U.S. officials "have adopted the label applied to rebels by the Colombian police and military—narcoterrorists."[5] In an earlier time it was the Malaysians, the Kenyans, the Angolans, the Argentinians, and, no less, the Jews resisting the British Mandate in Palestine. In the last half century U.S. forces and their accomplices have been burning and slaughtering "terrorists" in Korea, Vietnam, Nicaragua, Iraq, and elsewhere.

Definitional control can work by omission, as well as providing a framework for "understanding." For example, the framework can exclude the significant and focus on the trivial. In the United States this practice has been elevated to an art form. The annual special issue of *Time* magazine that features "the most influential people in America 1997" is richly illustrative.

One might be led to believe that this account would offer at least a glimpse of governing power in the United States. But *Time* qualifies its report at the outset, stating that its selectees "don't necessarily have the maximum in raw power." Instead, the magazine informs, "they have got other people to follow their lead.... Powerful people twist your arm. Influentials just sway your thinking."[6]

With this facile distinction, *Time* steers its readers' attention away from power and toward style and personality, while still creating the impression that it is revealing how the country is run. *Time*'s roster of most influential Americans begins with the twenty-one-year-old Tiger Woods, the phenomenal new golfing star, and includes, among others, Secretary of State Madeleine Albright, U.S. Senator John McCain, radio talk show host Don Imus, black scholar Henry Louis Gates, Jr., Miramax

Films chairman Harvey Weinstein, an economist, a product designer, a pop musician, a TV talk show host, a mutual funds manager, the editor of the unspeakably debased *National Enquirer*, the billionaire speculator and philanthropist George Soros, and Colin Powell.

To complete the list, there are two individuals with significant ties to real power: Richard Mellon Scaife, heir to part of the Mellon money and financial angel to many ultraconservative organizations and causes, and Robert Rubin, secretary of the treasury and former co-manager of the powerful Wall Street firm Goldman, Sachs, Inc. Yet these two exceptions are individuals now separated from the power clusters that gave them their personal wealth.

Time's listing confers authority mostly on service providers, not on the sources and wielders of genuine power in the country. From this list, readers can feel informed while actually remaining ignorant of the realities of power in America. Far more useful for getting a sense of this reality, for example, was a table published a month later in the back business pages of *The New York Times,* listing the ten largest U.S. goods and service-producing corporations by market capitalization. Heading the list was General Electric, followed by Coca-Cola, Exxon, Microsoft, Intel, Merck, Philip Morris, Procter & Gamble, IBM, and Johnson & Johnson.

How much more enlightened *Time*'s readership might have been if these corporations and their CEOs had headed its list of influentials. The briefest descriptions of what these companies do, where they are located (home and abroad), what decisions they make about investment and labor, and how these decisions affect people in and outside the United States would offer a critical dimension for assessing the real distribution of power, here and overseas.

A NEW BREED OF WELL-FINANCED IDEOLOGISTS

But such information, in context, is precisely what definitional control is employed to prevent. Besides, there has emerged in recent decades a new galaxy of information producers and analysts whose task is to obscure and shield the wielders of power from public attention. These are the very conservative institutes, research organizations, and think tanks that prepare studies on legal, social, and economic issues from a propertied and corporate perspective. This is to be expected; the corporate sector is the source of their funds.

Giving themselves either neutral, or seemingly public interest-sounding names, these organizations and their staff professionals turn out a sizable quantity of studies and reports that are given full credibility in the national and local informational circuits. Right-wing think tankers enjoy wide and hospitable access to local radio as well as national TV, and they lobby quietly with local, state, and national officials.

The Manhattan Institute in New York City is such an outfit. Its mission, as described by its president, is "to develop ideas and get them into mainstream circulation—with the help of 'the media food chain.'" Acccordingly, several times a month, the institute hosts "discreetly lavish public-policy lunches... to which it invites hundreds of journalists, politicians, bureaucrats, business people, and foundation staff members to hear a speaker on a subject the institute likes." This kind of cozy forum, reports *The New York Times,* "has nudged New York to the right."[7]

The institute has had plenty of backup and reinforcement from other like-minded organizations. But the essential point about this, and dozens of similar organizations, is that they provide public conduits for the corporate voice, itself by no means a whisper in the land. A consequence of this relatively recent—notable in the last few decades—phenomenon is that the public's information well becomes polluted at the source. And in this activity too, the United States is far in the lead.

MARKET RULES AND CULTURAL DEPRIVATION

Yet these are visible structures of ideology creation and dissemination. Far more effective, and not nearly as visible, in achieving definitional control are the dynamics of the market system itself, especially as they relate to the conscious-creating cultural industries—film, TV, music, publishing, and a variety of entertainments. These industries have provided incalculable support to U.S. corporate influence domestically and its expansion globally.

Here the focus is not on cultural industries' external impact, but on how their economic strength, political authority, and cultural power, utilizing market rules and values, have affected the American public. A popular north-of-the-(U.S.) border radio host looked at this influence from his Canadian observation post: "When I say this it is not in the spirit of anti-Americanism, but we live next door to the cultural monolith and it washes over us every day in every way."[8]

But it is this same monolith that washes over Americans first and foremost, and this is the locus of attention here. This is not to minimize the impacts abroad of American pop culture, serving as an advance promoter for U.S. corporate products and values. Yet it is indisputable that the impact of conglomeratized control of the cultural product falls first, and most heavily, on domestic audiences, viewers, listeners, and readers. And it is a grotesque irony that the nation whose leaders pronounce it the "greatest," and who regard other countries as pathetic examples of information and cultural deprivation, govern a people who are prevented from sampling the world's diverse creative output not by fiat, but by "market forces."

Only in exceptional cases are foreign cultural products forbidden entry into the United States. Sometimes a Cuban artist, or a writer from a country designated a "rogue" state by Washington, is excluded. But this kind of administrative censorship—though important and not infrequent—is insignificant in comparison with the far-reaching *structural* exclusion that characterizes the meager menu of foreign creative work reaching America.

A report about the accessibility of foreign films and video to domestic audiences states: "The three French films opening this month [December 1996]—bring to 55 the total of foreign language films released in 1996 in New York. Few Americans can name any of them. Fewer have gone to see them. In 1995, foreign films represented only 0.75 percent of the box office take."

The video film market—crucial to the economic viability of a movie today—hardly exists for foreign film. "Most [such] films never get beyond 10,000 to 15,000 copies on video... the average video store dedicates 1.2 percent of its space to foreign titles."[9] Compare American viewers' starvation diet of foreign films with audiences' options in Europe and most of the world, where screens are filled with U.S. movies.

What accounts for this wild imbalance? No single explanation is sufficient, but the sweeping expansion of "free trade" promoted by Washington since World War II is the central factor. This mislabeled trade relationship has enabled the strong U.S. cultural industries' products to overwhelm foreign cultural production. Foreign film production is at a terrific disadvantage in relation to U.S. film producers, who enjoy a large, unified, and relatively wealthy domestic market. The consequences have been calamitous for foreign film industries, reduced and marginalized in the global market. Foreign film directors and actors are sucked into Hollywood. Foreign audiences are scooped up by American $100-million special effects blockbusters, promoted with advertising budgets of $40 million dollars or more. The same fare gets its initial screening domestically. Foreign offerings, if they make it into the United States market at all, are increasingly made to satisfy audiences already shaped by their long-standing film experience with the Hollywood product.

In both situations—domestic and foreign—the filmgoer suffers, as the range of offerings is determined by corporate criteria of marketability and profitability. In the United States, the cultural deprivation is greater because the authority of Hollywood is uncontested and the market's exclusion of diversity more pervasive.

Yet if Americans rarely see a foreign film, their insulation from television made beyond their borders is greater still. With the exception of the British Broadcasting Corporation's carefully designed costume dramas of nineteenth-century country life, historical pageantry, Sherlock Holmes mysteries, and a few adaptations, produced for the relatively tiny audience of public broadcasting, a near total vacuum in dramatic programming from abroad prevails.

The growth of English as a global second language—a development of recent decades, accompanying the triumph of American pop culture globally—paradoxically further distances Americans from foreign media material and reinforces the domestic economy's near-hermetic cultural condition. If the film or TV program isn't in English, most Americans, the film industry avows, will be unwilling to read subtitles—and dubbing is either too expensive or inadequate. In either case, the spread of English operates to narrow, not broaden, the experience.

The familiarity of American readers with current world literature is no less abysmal. A distinguished American translator of European authors outlines this situation:

I was able to get hold of the records of PEN New York, which every year awards its PEN Translation Prize. All the publishing houses, from major conglomerates to mom-and-pop operations and university presses, submit works that have been translated from all the literatures of the world. We're not talking here about cookbooks or tour guides or auto mechanics, but about what a group of people, after a great deal of wrangling, decide is probably "literature." I presume that most of the serious prose and poetry that gets published in a given year is on PEN's list.

In any given year, at least over the the past five years, that list of published translations, from all the languages of the world, has not exceeded more than 200 to 250 titles. So every year we Americans are getting no more than about 200 peeks a year over the literary fence into the world outside.

Then, if you start looking at the individual languages, about 60 percent of the books are translated from five languages, and in this order: French, Spanish, German, Russian, Italian. So that's approximately 120 titles. All the rest of the world's languages get the other 80.[10]

The situation is hardly different as far as news is concerned. A couple of corporate giants, CNN and more recently CNBC, provide foreign TV coverage with an emphasis on breaking crises. The four major networks' reports are notable for their infrequency and tiny proportion of an already insubstantial overall time allocation (twenty-two minutes, or less, for total national news programming daily).

THE U.S. NEWS MEDIA

The American news ration, whatever the medium—newspapers, magazines, radio, or TV—is almost totally dependent on a handful of Western international news agencies: AP, Reuters, Agence France Press, and UPI. When the dominance of these agencies was briefly contested in the late 1960s and early 1970s, mostly by Third World leaders who argued for a "new international information order," their challenge was swept aside by Anglo-American leaders. The Third World concern with concentrated and monopolistic corporate control of the global news flow was dismissed by Washington and London as being an unacceptable endorsement of censorship and tyranny. It was on these grounds that the United States and Great Britain withdrew from UNESCO in the mid-1980s.

Since then, most of the messages and images of the world come from still greater concentrated private channels. A temporary exception is the Internet; this new communication resource has enabled some unconventional expression—e.g., views of the Mexican rebels in Chiapas—to be circulated that otherwise would have faced unresponsive corporate-owned circuits. But on the whole, the capability to select what the American audience can see, hear, and read remains tightly administered by a tiny group of corporate media moguls. Their executives emphasize the splendid technologies for providing instantaneous attention to, and universal distribution of, the day's events. Who is interpreting these events, even in the initial step of selecting which of them is worth reporting, is left unattended.

Given these arrangements, it is hardly surprising that most Americans' knowledge of the world and its problems is less than microscopic. "Weapons of Mass Distraction" is the way one writer described the functioning of the media system, TV in particular, in the United States today. Larry Gelbart, who, as screenwriter, earlier wrote about the depredations of the tobacco industry in the movie *Barbarians at the Gate*, explained his new film: "Tobacco executives are only dangerous to smokers. But we all smoke the news. We all inhale television. We all subscribe to what these men are putting out. They're much more dangerous [than tobacco corporate executives]."[11]

The effects of this nutritionally deficient menu of news and general imagery, heavily seasoned with distraction—Versace's murder and Princess Diana's near canonization in the summer of 1997, the Bill Clinton sex soap opera in 1998—that Americans consume daily are observable in many otherwise hard-to-explain national characteristics. How, for example, to account for the dearth of heroes, other than sports figures or entertainment personalities, in the twentieth-century American pantheon? With the possible exception of Martin Luther King, Jr., those who resisted various features of the American Century (and there were, and are, many) have been screened out of the national consciousness.

That American familiarity with the world beyond the domestic shores of the Atlantic and Pacific is shockingly limited is burden enough for the development of knowledgeable people. Lack of awareness of one's own history, and ignorance about the individuals who have been some of the main, if unorthodox, voices, casts doubt on the very premise of citizenship.

In a recent interview with Pete Seeger in the *Los Angeles Times*, the reporter described Seeger, who has been singing publicly for more than sixty years and who was a colleague of Woody Guthrie, as "probably the individual most responsible for the popularity of folk music." Out of curiosity, I asked my class of thirty-nine senior students, most of them graduating in June 1997, if they knew anything about Pete Seeger. Not one had ever heard of him. This from a group at an elite research university, communication majors all.

How to explain it? Seeger offers this insight, albeit not to the question here: "There has never been any time in the last thirty years when folk songs have receded. They simply went off TV. Does that mean they receded?"[12]

Simply not appearing on TV in America today does in fact mean you don't exist for the national audience. And for this audience, a great number of people, events, social movements, and creative efforts do not exist because they are not on TV screens. The American state of ignorance of the rest of the world has been extended since the end of the Cold War and the emergence of the United States as a self-satisfied and unchallenged superpower. A study of TV coverage of foreign events on nightly national news programs—the main source of information for the public—strikingly demonstrates this:

> The number and length of foreign topics in the evening news have declined far below Cold War levels. As a percentage of all topics covered between 1970 and 1995, the share of foreign stories fell from 35 percent to 23 percent, and the average length of these stories dropped from 1.7 minutes to 1.2 minutes. Worse, while the networks devoted on average more than 40 percent of total news time to foreign items in the 1970s, that share had been cut to 13.5 percent of news time by 1995.

The writer concludes, "Among the enormous offerings of cable and satellite television... foreign news in particular [is] disappearing in a flood of entertainment and niche-oriented channels."[13]

This condition has not passed totally unnoticed. The TV critic of the *Los Angeles Times* ruminated, "The United States sees itself largely as the throbbing, pulsating epicenter of sentient life, a lush, green oasis in a barren moonscape, and expects to remain so evermore... the less coverage of the rest of the globe, the more disconnected we feel."[14]

But TV is not a complete vacuum. There is *something* on the screen that people watch for several hours a day. And this something is contributing heavily to what Norwegian political scientist Johann Galtung terms the TV idiotization of Americans. TV news, for example, never free of dollops of ideology in the past, has now become so commoditized that it chooses most of its content for its entertainment value, in quest of the large audience.

An account of local news-gathering in Los Angeles, the second most influential media center after New York City, offers this example: "Cutthroat competition among the city's nine TV stations and four radio news shows means as many as thirteen full-time 'mediaships' [helicopters] may be cruising for news at all hours of the day. And on slow days, critics say, the 'news' turns into thin stories plucked from the air: sick dolphins, gushing fire hydrants or, worse, events hyped well beyond their newsworthiness." To compound the condition, the report adds that "many TV stations [across the country] are looking to Los Angeles as the model for the new profession of pilot-reporters."[15]

THE MARKETING ROLE OF THE UNITED STATES' INFORMATION SYSTEM

Yet the national ignorance cannot be accounted for solely by the trivialization and withholding of news. It has much deeper roots. The structural foundation of the media system, and its unrestrained market-determined operations, financed exclusively by those who can afford to buy time and messages, assure a continuing cultural impoverishment of the audience. As the giant goods-and-services-producing corporations account for the bulk of all the media's financial support, it is their messages, many billions' worth annually for TV alone, that create the all-embracing commercial atmosphere in the country.

As such, inadequate and trivialized news is only part of the public's information problem. Its saturation with commercial messages is another. Few have attempted to measure the impact on individuals of the incessant flow of commercials. Though this may seem curious, it can be explained by the low priority of such research for those with the funds to finance it—the companies actually making the advertising expenditures. This does not mean that the companies ignore the impact of advertising. The studies that they do support are first of all, proprietary. They are privately owned and witheld from the public.

Additionally, corporate interest in what commercials do to those who are absorbing them is nil. Corporate concern is over whether the commercials are effective. The creative director of one New York advertising agency explained, "No one's really worrying about what it's teaching impressionable youth. Hey, I'm in the business of convincing people to buy things they don't need."[16]

This perverse condition provides another aspect of what it means to be living in the center of the global corporate system. No people in the world are subject to as heavy a barrage of commercial imagery and messages as Americans. In recent years, as the corporate marketing system grows increasingly global, other nations are experiencing rising advertising expenditures per capita—and these are almost certain to accelerate.

All the same, the United States, as the strongest force in and the greatest proponent of the marketing system, remains in a class by itself in the production and dissemination of advertising commercials in all media and into all possible spaces, public and private.

What precisely this means is difficult to specify, but to assume there is no effect on the people caught in the center of this commercial onslaught is to be willfully blind. At the very least, it suggests distraction, confusion, absorption with consumption, fragmented attention, out-of-alignment social priorities—or all of the above. Perhaps the all-encompassing commercial environment has become part of Americans' DNA. Certainly noncommercial culture has had a precarious existence, though dedicated and talented people have worked arduously on its behalf. Historically, the country lacks a public service broadcasting tradition. The larger public has never experienced anything but a thoroughly commercial system from its outset in the 1920s, except for a few failed attempts to create a publicly accountable broadcasting.[17] The one exception has been the government-subsidized arts in the Great Depression. Commercial culture has become accepted as the natural order of information production and distribution. Other systems are either unknown to most Americans or are rejected as "statist."

The commercial pummeling of the American mind begins at a very early age, generally coincident with a youngster's ability to focus on a moving image. Here again, studies by noncommercial researchers on the impact of incessant advertising on preschool and preteen children are either limited or nonexistent.

Yet the situation is so gross that *Business Week*, a publication not known for its hostility to the market economy, has been prompted to publish a cover story, "Hey Kid, Buy This," asking rhetorically, "Is Madison Avenue taking 'Get 'em while they're young' too far?" The report chronicles the depredations imposed on the country's tots unsentimentally:

> At 1:58 P.M. on Wednesday, May 5 [1997] a consumer was born.... by the time she went home three days later, some of America's biggest marketers were pursuing her with samples, coupons, and assorted freebies.... Like no generation before, [she] enters a consumer culture surrounded by logos, labels, and ads almost from the moment of birth.... By the time she's twenty months old, she will start to recognize some of the thousands of brands flashed in front of her each day. At age seven, if she's anything like the typical kid, she will see some 20,000 TV commercials a year. By the time she's twelve, she will have her own entry in the massive databases of marketers.[18]

If this is not sufficient cause for public outrage, consider what is occurring on the Internet, the network that is supposed to provide information and cultural treasures to the kiddies, if Vice President Gore and President Clinton are to be believed. In a report subtitled "How Business Pumps Kids on Web," we are informed, "As millions of kids go online, marketers are in hot pursuit. Eager to reach an enthusiastic audience more open to [sales] pitches than the typical adult buried in junk mail, companies often entertain tykes online with games and contests. But to play, these sites frequently require children to fill out questionaires about themselves and their families and friends—valuable data to be sorted and stored in marketing databases."[19]

Business Week, after describing the process in its ugliest details, agonizes about the marketing web spun around the nation's kids, acknowledging that "the cumulative effect of initiating our children into a consumerist ethos at an ever earlier age may be profound."[20] Yet it gives the usual anodyne solution to the systemic cancer it has revealed. It recommends parental responsibility to protect the children against this malevolent atmosphere. Could one expect it to propose changes in the corporate order that produces this condition?

The "cumulative effects" of unbridled commercialism, however difficult to assess, constitute one key to the impact of growing up in the core of the world's marketing system. Minimally, it suggests unpreparedness for, and lack of interest in, the world that exists outside the shopping mall.

INCREASING CONSERVATIVE INFLUENCE ON MEDIA INSTITUTIONS

While learning about and preparing for shopping can be a lifetime pursuit in itself, U.S. shoppers do have to drive to the malls and take their cars out for work or show. When they do this, they cannot escape not only more commercial messages but round-the-clock salvos from the "know nothing" radio hosts who now dominate the airwaves. The quality of media information in the days of newspaper primacy may have left a lot to be desired, but in the 1990s, radio, and to an increasing extent TV, have been taken over to express the views of a substantial but minority conservatism.

Recent decades have seen a tremendous growth in private corporate wealth and individual rich stockholders. In this now unimaginably affluent sector of the social order, a hard-line conservative component views social welfare institutions that developed in the last century as temporary aberrations, to be eliminated as quickly as possible. This already powerful and growing contingent has used its great wealth to attract and mobilize large numbers of capable individuals to do battle in the media-informational and political spheres. They work directly in existing media institutions or in creating new forms that serve as pressure agents on the national informational apparatus: the schools, churches, civic and social organizations, and media.

Suggestive of the dimensions of this reactionary force in the body politic is the expanding role of a number of conservative foundations whose main purpose is to finance a variety of institutions created to influence public opinion and state policy. Dozens of tax-exempt institutes and think tanks have proliferated in the last several years, organizing forums, releasing studies and reports, and most effectively, offering speakers and "experts" to remarkably receptive radio and TV programs and panels:

Major news media continued to give greater prominence to conservative think tanks in 1996 [reported] a survey of major paper and broadcast media citations in the Nexis computer database. Of the ten most media-cited think tanks, six are conservative or right-leaning, three are centrist, and one is left-leaning. More than half of the total citations of think tanks were to conservative or right-leaning institutions: only 13 percent cited progressive or left-leaning institutions.

The top four think tanks cited in the media were:
Brookings Institution—centrist 2,220 citations
Heritage Foundation—conservative 2,086
American Enterprise Institute—conservative 1,417
Cato Institute—conservative libertarian 1,145[21]

A 1997 report from the National Committee for Responsive Philanthropy noted that "conservative foundations are playing a major role in shaping public policy priorities." From 1992 to 1994, "twelve conservative foundations—including the Bradley, Scaife, and Olin foundations—controlled assets of $1.1 billion and awarded $300 million in grants." The report acknowledged that these sums are relatively modest in comparison with the nation's biggest foundations, but it emphasized that the grant-giving practices of the conservative organizations are concentrated on national policy objectives and targeted on institutions that are "extremely aggressive and ideological."[22]

But this activity has to be seen in a larger context. It is not as if the old-line foundations were funding institutions advocating radical social change and the right-wingers were mounting a defensive counterattack. The large conventional foundations— Ford, Rockefeller, Carnegie, and so on—overwhelmingly support status quo institutions and activities. The conservative money is going to those who are intent on pushing the social order to the right.

Not all the reactionary outfits are smooth and savvy. Yet all contribute to a local and national environment in which people are pushed to accept the destruction of values, practices, and institutions that have constituted the humane and democratic aspirations of the nation.

One of the primary targets of the allegedly publicly concerned groups is government. Certainly the interventionist policies of the U.S. government over the fifty-year period since the end of World War II cannot be defended, since these policies have been pursued in the interests of the governing corporate class. But the currently vociferous opponents of government do not mention these activities. Instead they claim that government as a form of political organization is intolerable. This is not the principled position of anarchism, but the thinly veiled apologetics for private, corporate direction of the country. Encountering these sentiments in hundreds of channels daily, the public cannot possibly begin to understand, much less deal with, the urgent issues of local, national, or international existence.

In international affairs, there is a rich record for the last half century of American interventions against popular governments and in support of right-wing regimes. In many of these sordid episodes, the United Nations has been either ignored or pressured into acquiescence. Still, the international organization, for all its weaknesses, lapses, and subservience to Washington, represents the possibility of a world organized on equitable and humane principles—a potential that is the object of the scorn and near-fanatical hostility of hard-line conservatives. The public is exposed to ceaseless tirades from large sections of complicit media against the very idea of a United Nations, invective that penetrates the mainstream media as well. Subject to a decades-long campaign, the U.S. public, or at least a considerable part of it, has been inculcated with suspicion and fear of the United Nations and related international bodies like UNESCO or the World Health Organization. Organizations directly, or largely, under U.S. fiat, such as the International Monetary Fund or NATO, generally escape such criticism. When the International Monetary Fund is criticized by the right, it is because *any* joint international activity is viewed suspiciously; its preference is for unilateral action.

It is not that the United Nations and its related bodies are above criticism. But it is their *functions* that are attacked as threatening and unnecessary. Here too Washington, which has been ordering around much of the world for fifty years, speaks for a population, a good part of which knows nothing and cares less about its leaders' actions in these spheres. Instead it is fed, and accepts, a condemnation of the principles of international solidarity.

How otherwise to explain the continuing harassment of the UN by U.S. politicians with the complicity of the national media? The American public's untroubled acceptance of a now decades-old condition in which one nation—its own—dictates the policies and administrative organization of an enterprise with two hundred member states is a striking example of the clouds of deception that envelop consciousness in the center of the global economy.

The most rudimentary understanding of and empathy for the need of mutuality among nations would reject out of hand such chauvinistic and unilateralist behavior. Lamentably, both these qualities—understanding and empathy—are in short supply in the United States today, victims of unrelenting attack. And it is not only the UN and the international community that suffer. Americans made less concerned with others and more concerned with self, turn away from their own weak and poor as well, and adopt the rationales of those who see no need for protective social networks.

CONCLUSION

How long will the now unchallenged superpower retain its ascendancy? A great effort is being made to maximize what is currently the strongest component of American world influence: its information and cultural power. One observer, sympathetic to

American global preeminence, sees it as a longlasting condition: "it is far harder to foresee a turnaround in the fundamentals of American soft power [the informational-mass cultural sphere]"[23]

Daily accounts from around the world seem to sustain this view: "Worldwide MTV claims 281 million viewing households with 66 million in the U.S. plus more than 20 million in Latin America and about 50 million in Asia." The report sees a "Global Mall" with youths "flush with cash and plastic… look[ing] upon Levis and tune[ing] in to MTV."[24] In fall 1998 the *Washington Post* published an extensive three-part series of reports, headlined "American Pop Penetrates World," detailing the takeover of global culture by American product.[25]

The acceptance—though there are some points of resistance—of the American consumerist privatized model abroad strengthens the prevailing domestic mindset and the myopic views that accompany it. Actually, the export "model" is shot through with failings, the most important of which is that only about 15 percent, at most 25 percent, of the people in what Wall Street euphemistically calls the "emerging markets" participate in the new consumption standard. The rest are window-shoppers at best, while the numbers of destitute grow larger. This side of the story gets minimum attention.

When, for example, former Mexican president Salinas de Gortari imposed the American model on his country in the late 1980s, he received celebrity treatment in the U.S. media. The news of the collapse of the Mexican peso a few years later, and the massive unemployment that followed, as they were reported, inadequately and out of context in the U.S. press, did little to inform, to say nothing of educate, Americans about what had happened and why.

Edward Said, in his book *Culture and Imperialism*, observes that the European colonialists, however commanding and brutal, were always aware that they were imperialists.[26] This cannot be said of the American brand of order giving. The market mechanism—the relatively invisible mechanisms of finance, trade, and investment, all seen as part of a free market and a free world—denies the existence of unequal relations between states and peoples and lends credibility to the governing class's rhetoric of freedom.

Only the most profound shocks in the global and domestic economies will be sufficient to shake the beliefs and values that now prevail in the minds and consciousnesses of most Americans. This is not a comforting thought. But the machinery of mind management is so entrenched and pervasive that nothing less than seismic movements can be expected to loosen or weaken its pernicious authority.

NOTES

1. *The New York Times Magazine,* June 7, 1997, 37.

2. Michael Janofsky, "Delegates Hope to Prolong Volunteer Spirit," *The New York Times,* April 30, 1997, A-10.

3. David Rothkopf, "In Praise of Cultural Imperialism?", *Foreign Policy,* no. 107 (Summer 1997): 48–49.

4. Diana Jean Schemo, "As a Rebel's Path Ends, Hard Turf but Soft Hearts," *The New York Times,* April 29, 1997.

5. Remarks by U.S. Secretary of State Madeleine K. Albright, National Press Club, Washington, D.C., August 6, 1997, in *The New York Times*, August 8, 1997, 12–13; and Diana Jean Schemo, "Congress Steps Up Aid for Colombia to Combat Drugs," *The New York Times*, December 1, 1998, 1.

6. "*Time*'s Most Influential Americans," *Time* 149, no. 16 (April 21, 1997): 40–67.

7. Janny Scott, "Intellectuals Who Became Influential," *The New York Times*, May l2, 1997, A-13.

8. Anthony De Palma, "After 27,000 Guests, the Great Gabfest Winds Up," *The New York Times*, May 22, 1997.

9. Linda Lee, "Nobody Reads a Good Movie These Days," *The New York Times*, December 9, 1996, C-7.

10. John E. Woods, *San Diego Weekly Reader* 26, no. 32 (August 14, 1997): 20–22.

11. Frank Rich, "Mad As Hell," *The New York Times,* May 8, 1997, A-23.

12. *Los Angeles Times*, May 20, 1997.

13. Claude Moisy, "Myths of the Global Information Village," *Foreign Policy,* no. 107 (Summer 1997): 82.

14. Howard Rosenberg, "Foreign News? It's All Alien to the Networks," *Los Angeles Times*, May 30, 1997, F-1.

15. Lisa Bannon, "In TV Chopper Wars, News is Sometimes a Trivial Pursuit," *Wall Street Journal,* June 4, 1997, 1.

16. Thomas Bartlett, "Two for Me, None for You," *Business Week*, August 11, 1997, 35.

17. Robert McChesney, *Telecommunications, Mass Media and Democracy* (New York: Oxford University Press, 1993).

18. "Hey Kid, Buy This," *Business Week,* June 30, 1997, 61–69.

19. Jared Sandberg, "Ply and Pry: How Business Pumps Kids on Web," *Wall Street Journal,* June 9, 1997, B-1.

20. "Hey Kid, Buy This."

21. Michael Dolny, "New Survey on Think Tanks," *Extra,* July/August 1997.

22. National Committee for Responsive Philanthropy, "Moving a Public Policy Agenda: The Strategic Philanthropy of Conservative Foundations," Washington, D.C., July 2, 1997.

23. Josef Joffe, "America the Inescapable," *The New York Times Magazine,* June 8, 1997, 43.

24. Bernard Wysocki, Jr., "The Global Mall," *Wall Street Journal,* June 26, 1997, 1.

25. "American Pop Penetrates World," part 1 of 3-part series, *Washington Post,* October 25, 26, and 27, 1998.

26. Edward W. Said, *Culture and Imperialism* (New York: Knopf, 1993).

CHAPTER SEVEN

NUMBER ONE IN THE TWENTY-FIRST CENTURY

Can the extraordinary influence that the United States has exercised in world affairs over the last fifty-five years be maintained in the new century? Many in the higher circles of power seem to think so. Some give great weight to the technological lead the United States still enjoys, especially in electronic industries. There are also gloomier assessments.

Historical experience tells us that all empires end, some sooner than others. The signs are multiplying that Numero Uno's position of global dominance is beginning to weaken. Actually, markers have been observable since the early 1970s, but the relatively boom years of the 1990s have somewhat obscured them. No cave-ins yet, and sagging bulwarks can be reinforced up to a point, but still, the stresses are unmistakably present. The pressures are external and domestic.

INTERNATIONAL PRESSURE ON U.S. PRIMACY

One growing threat to the stability of the U.S. economy, and therefore to its capability to continue to direct the global order, paradoxically emerges from its success in establishing capitalism around the world.

Since the end of World War II, American policy did everything in its considerable power to stop new and old nations from adopting noncapitalist systems. To achieve this, no means—financial, political, military—was excluded to prevent what at that time were likely eventualities. The editor of *Foreign Affairs* put it this way: "We have cajoled, urged, bribed, and threatened regimes to liberalize their economies along Anglo-American lines."[1]

Not only were countries coerced into relinquishing their hopes and designs for alternative ways of living, but those relatively few places that had embarked on a different course were forced to heel and abandon their varying socialist projects.

By the time the Soviet Union disintegrated as a sovereign state, what was once called, to no one's satisfaction, the Third World—the aggregation of ex-colonial states and the dependent economies of Latin America—had also ceased to exist, transmogrified into investor-designated "emerging market" societies. These are the same still relatively poor and weak states discovered by Wall Street as potential outlets for the huge capital accumulations piled up in the public and private treasuries of the rich nations. It is this group of countries that has been dragooned into the world capitalist economy.

For the moment, this neat magician's trick can only be seen as a stunning victory for U.S. capitalism and its postwar policy. Yet within a few years, what seemed such a triumph has revealed an unexpected, and menacing, vulnerability. Capitalism, systemically afflicted by crisis, has extended the locus of crisis to the entire world, and most notably to many economies with extremely weak underpinnings.

This might be regarded as just another burden placed on those with the least power to sustain themselves, but, valid as this conclusion is, it misses a larger issue. The organization of the world market system by transnational capital in recent decades has encouraged massive capital flows into many of the former Third World states—Malaysia, Thailand, Indonesia, Brazil, Mexico—and also into Russia, now very much resembling a poor, dependent country.

What begins as a crisis in one of the "emerging markets," facilitated by advanced electronic networks and the mobility of capital that they enable, can move rapidly through the entire system. The Asian crisis, beginning in mid-1997 in Thailand, spread across the region and moved into Russia and Latin America in short order. Each of these areas, separately, had been sucked up into a familiar speculative bubble, making it especially susceptible to shocks elsewhere in the system. This is an example of what may be expected with some regularity.

But the consequences don't stop at the borders of the directly affected states. The United States, still the center of the system, finds itself pressed on two sides: it must safeguard its own economy, and at the same time, in its self-interest as empire overseer, it must use its own resources to bail out the stricken areas, which have become inextricably tied to the world financial and economic order. In the recent crisis, South Korea, Indonesia, Brazil, and Russia became claimants for huge special assistance programs. These calls on the U.S. Treasury, likely to be recurring, cannot fail to be a huge strain on Numero Uno's general strength and capacity to run the world system. This accounts in part for the emphasis in U.S. governmental and financial centers on expanding the resources of the International Monetary Fund, thereby pooling the risk.

At the same time, as this stress becomes a likely permanent feature of America's world power position, a newcomer in the international arena, the euro, is rising to challenge the ultimate emblem of American supremacy—the U.S. dollar. With the arrival of the euro on January 4, 1999, as the standard currency of the European Community (Euroland), a rival economic bloc asserts its intention to do battle with the dollar. It is a force to be reckoned with. In 1997 the value of Euroland's gross product was $6.28 trillion, compared with $8.09 trillion for the United States.[2]

The euro, the new currency of the eleven countries presently comprising Euroland, is already seen, perhaps prematurely, as a threat to the U.S. dollar. What is involved here is not merely a matter of prestige. Substantial material benefits accrue to the currency that attains global primacy. "The nation, or nations, whose currency prevails," writes one observer, "will enjoy lower interest rates on government debt, cheaper financing and transaction costs for business, competitive advantages for banks and other financial institutions, a spur for economic growth and enhanced political power."[3] Remember, too, that these advantages always accrue to the already most powerful state. This makes its position still more weighty in the world arena.

A loss of the dollar's world supremacy, if it occurs, will represent far more than the diminution of economic benefits, significant as these are. "It would mean," writes *Wall Street Journal* correspondent Michael Sesit, "that Europe after fifty-four years, has emancipated itself from the American financial hegemony under which it fell at the end of World War II." More portentous still, another prediction claims that "the death of the dollar order will drastically increase the price of the American dream, while simultaneously shattering American global influence."[4]

An inkling of what may be coming shows in two brief press reports in November 1998. One announces a trip of the president of the European Commission to China, its purpose to "encourage China to use the euro, to be introduced on January 1 [1999], as an alternative to the dollar as a reserve currency and means of financing foreign debt."[5] A second story, more speculative, attributes the dollar's weakness in the fall of 1998 to "Japanese institutions' liquidating dollar holdings in exchange for the euro."[6] The euro has yet to demonstrate its viability, but if it falls short, there cannot fail to be other long-term contenders. How this will play out is uncertain at best. For the moment, the dollar remains the world's preferred currency.

In any case, the dollar's well-being will not be exclusively dependent on the strength or weakness of the euro or any other currency. There are other factors. One is the huge U.S. annual trade deficit that creates additional strains on the country's world position and its currency. For many years after World War II, Washington lectured and economically hectored those nations that ran deficits in their foreign trade. England, for example, was frequently a recipient of this treatment. Over the years, dozens of other countries received similar sermons, reinforced by U.S. economic pressure. Yet their deficits were minuscule when compared with the negative balances piled up by the United States in recent years, largely as a result of unbridled domestic consumption and the necessity of importing goods from the struggling states in the imperial periphery.

These deficits are sums owed to the creditor export nations and are paid for with U.S. dollars. When the United States runs a $220 billion or more trade deficit, as it did in 1998, U.S.$220 billion flow out of the country to pay the balance. How long will foreign exporters and their banks be content to hold U.S. dollars? This was never in question during the period of Numero Uno's ascendancy, but it is now. These foreign-held U.S. dollars represent gigantic loans to the United States.

There is no time limit that fixes the willingness of foreigners to hold U.S. currency. It is the general acceptability of the dollar that is determining. Developments that weaken the overall U.S. economy affect the strength of the dollar and its continued acceptance as a reserve currency. In Lester Thurow's *Future of Capitalism,* published a few years ago, the former dean of MIT's School of Management states flatly, "No country, not even one as big as the United States, can run a trade deficit forever.... The question is not whether an earthquake will occur. It will. The only question is when."[7]

It is indisputable that U.S. economic, technological, military, and pop cultural strength remain formidable. But each of these areas has its problems. The custodians of U.S. power can hardly be sanguine about the time ahead. The 1997–98 Asian economic crisis provided a foretaste of what the future may bring. In the fall of 1997, at the annual meetings of the International Monetary Fund (IMF) and the World Bank, Japan offered a plan, one which excluded the United States, to raise substantial funds for the stricken countries in the region. The *Wall Street Journal* reported the U.S. reaction:

> The sum was immense, but Mr. Rubin [U.S. Secretary of the Treasury] and Mr. Summers [Rubin's deputy] feared the fund would offer big loans with less-stringent conditions than the IMF's and would *threaten U.S. economic supremacy....* In drafting sessions and corridor conversations, Mr. Summers deftly put an end to Japan's Asia-centric proposal.... [And] a victorious Mr. Summers declared afterward, "U.S. economic leadership is crucial to avoid a descent into the kind of regionalism and protectionism that we saw in the periods between the first and second World Wars." (emphasis mine)[8]

The United States prevailed in this instance, but the crisis deepened and generated widespread attacks on the American-dominated International Monetary Fund and World Bank. For half a century these institutions, with dependence on the United States structured into their voting arrangements, have decided the policies that countries seeking aid and loans would have to follow. Complaints and criticisms from many poor borrowers were frequent, but the main industrial economies, and the U.S. in particular, paid no attention. The Asian crisis, extending across a huge continent and affecting many countries in the Western industrial core area as well, has put an end to this indifference.

Somewhat tardily, after fifty years' documented experience, it is now recognized and acknowledged in the Western media that the IMF, ostensibly an international body, is run by the United States. Since the onset of the crisis in Asia, the domestic media has offered the public an unfamiliar perspective. A *New York Times* writer, for example, reported, "Everywhere else in the world... politicans and businessmen insist that one of the biggest problems with the IMF is that, contrary to the view of Congress, it acts as the United States Treasury's lap dog." In the same account, an illustration of this charge is detailed:

> The bailouts of Russia and South Korea were prime examples of how Washington muscles into the Fund's [IMF] turf as soon as major American strategic interests are involved. Last Christmas, as South Korea slipped within days of running out of hard currency,... it sent a secret envoy, Kim Kihwan, to work out a rescue

package. "I didn't bother going to the IMF," Mr. Kim recalled recently. "I called Mr. Summers's office at the Treasury from my home in Seoul, flew to Washington, and went directly there. I knew that was how this would get done.[9]

He was right.

In the wake of the economic shocks of 1997–98, and the unusual publicly aired criticism of its American domination, the IMF is not likely to long remain the sovereign fiefdom of U.S. economic interests. Proposals from European countries for revamping the organization's decision-making structure have begun to circulate.[10]

Whatever changes are eventually made in the IMF's procedures, one outcome seems assured: the preponderant role of the United States in that body's decisions will be reduced. A major instrument in the machinery of U.S. global dominance will be less effective. Taken together with a challenged dollar and wider claims of troubled economies for U.S. assistance, American economic interests will be finding their global authority and influence pared down.

One means to counter this powerful set of forces now at work weakening Numero Uno's primacy, breathtaking in its simplistic and myopic view of the threats confronting that primacy, has been the decision in the fall of 1998 to "beef up" the CIA. The director, having received presidential approval and a congressional infusion of billions of dollars for the organization's expansion, will proceed, according to a published account, "to build up the agency's clandestine service of spies, open more overseas stations, undertake more covert operations, hire more in-house experts, buy faster and better computers, and bring in a new generation of recruits."[11]

How these measures will strengthen the U.S. economy and its world standing is left unclear.

THE SITUATION AT HOME

If the international prospect for continued U.S. superpower-dom and its prerogatives grows steadily more uncertain, no compensatory good news may be expected from domestic developments.

Despite the unremitting assurances from governing levels that the "fundamentals [of the American economy] remain strong," the problems that beset the social order are grave, numerous, intensifying, and deep-rooted in the system. Here three of these basic problems, which cannot avoid resulting eventually in a profound instability of the economy, are noted. These are (1) the continuing growth of inequality in the distribution of income; (2) the corporatization and commodification of all facets of life; and (3) a near-pathological promotion of consumerism. These conditions constitute the daily environment that everyone experiences, albeit with differing impacts, to be sure.

INEQUALITY OF INCOME

One of the defining characteristics of a market-based society is inequality in the distribution of the economy's production of goods and services, and consequently in the social relationships affected by differing material holdings—education, housing, health care, and cultural enjoyments. There is no demonstrable level at which an unequal distribution of resources creates tension and instability in the social order; many variables come into play. Yet one conclusion seems justified: the greater the economic inequality in a country, the less stable its political condition is likely to be. This becomes apparent to most, however, only after a social explosion occurs.

Given its market character since its origins, economic inequality always has been present in the United States. Yet with the exception of the years when industry was rapidly expanding and grossly exploiting the labor force in the 1870s and 1880s, and again in the depth of the Great Depression in the early 1930s, marked political instability, despite the presence of considerable economic inequality, has not been a significant factor in American life. This too may be changing.

In the first five years of the 1990s, a number of studies have documented the growth of economic inequality in the nation. In 1996, for example, a U.S. Census Bureau report, "A Brief Look at Postwar U.S. Economic Inequality," noted that the gap between the most affluent Americans and everyone else was wider than it has been since the end of World War II. In the twenty-five years, 1968–94, the report found that "the share of the nation's aggregate income that went to the top 20 percent of its households increased to 46.9 percent from 40.5 percent. During the same time, the share of income earned by the rest of the country's households either declined or remained stagnant."[12]

Another study, focusing on wealth, not annual income, reported a similar trend for a shorter period. It found that "the most prosperous 10 percent of American households held 61.1 percent of the nation's wealth in 1989 and 66.8 percent in late 1994."[13] This data extends only to 1994. In the five years since, a colossal rise on the American stock markets has added literally trillions of dollars to the assets of American shareholders, by and large the country's top earners and wealth holders. It is almost certain, therefore, that the growing income gaps and wealth disparities noted in the mid-1990s have deepened and widened since then.

A large, though decidedly minority, middle stratum in the United States, enjoying a booming affluence, serves to deflect attention from the conditions affecting the majority. Yet the inequality makes itself felt throughout the social sphere. Test scores reveal more about the differentials in students' housing and school amenities than natural talent. Millions of Americans can't pay for health services. The number of children living in families below the poverty line runs into the millions and continues to increase.

Inequality is most readily apparent in America's vast service sector. In education, entertainment, health services, sports, transportation, and housing, unequal treatment, and sometimes exclusion, of users (patients, travelers, fans, students, householders) whose incomes differ is now taken for granted.

But beyond the social distress that economic inequality

produces, there is a still more perilous condition that it sooner or later provokes—its effect on the stability of the economy. The unequal distribution of income is the chief source of the periodic crises that regularly erupt. This is generally concealed in conventional economics by reference to an unexplained lack of demand. A deepening inequality of income cannot fail eventually to produce a full-blown economic crisis, with unpredictable consequences for long-term survival of Numero Uno's status.

CORPORATIZATION AND COMMODIFICATION

While inequality scars ever more routines of daily life in America, and represents a time bomb under the economy, another feature of the times is the ongoing corporatization of the economy. This has been underway for decades but is now reaching out to spheres hitherto insulated from its embrace. Few are the activities today that are not organized by corporate entities. Most of the country's production and distribution have long been in corporate hands; now culture and human services—health care, education, the arts, and urban functions—are being taken over by corporate enterprise.

In this recent period, corporate holdings have been merged and combined at a staggering rate. Today huge concentrations of the country's economic and cultural resources are in the possession of a tiny number of private controllers.

The consequences of this awesome concentration of power are experienced, though not necessarily identified, in every

American household. They are present, though generally invisible, in the expansion or decay of communities; in the types and availabilities of jobs; in the health and longevity of the population; in the condition of the local schools; in the well-being of the environment; and in the kind of products and services on sale. The decisions taken, directly or indirectly, by remote corporate directors vitally affect everyone.

Equally consequential, the political process, which is supposed to be the means of making these decisions that are now largely in corporate hands, has been reduced to supplication for corporate financing. The electoral process has become a clear channel for corporate favor. Not every big business demand is satisfied, but the main ones are taken care of.

This condition is now so pervasive that public awareness of it is widespread, contributing yet another element of potential instability to the national atmosphere. The erosion of the democratic process by the concentration of enormous economic power in relatively few private hands is at a very advanced stage.

Less tangible, but no less perilous, the corporate quest for profitability has led to the commodification of most of the activities that people engage in. Human encounters in which social relationships have been transformed into commercial transactions are now the common experience. As the public sector in the United States is cut down and marginalized to suit the philosophy that only profit-making endeavors are beneficial, functions once public and social, that is, nonprofit, have been forced to commercialize, charge fees, and act as profit seekers.

Health services have been turned over to HMOs (health management organizations). Education is increasingly being privatized, and private enterpreneurs are busily moving in on public schools and colleges. Libraries, museums, national parks, and public theater are all caught in the iron demand of the bottom line. If present trends continue, all human interactions will be put on a pay-for basis. This denies the social nature of human existence and elevates self and selfishness as the primary motivators of people. In such an order, common or national endeavors have little chance of acceptance, and agreeable human associations disappear.

Reinforcing the increasing commercialization of social interactions, electronic technologies carry these developments still further. In their corporate application, they enable many services to dispense altogether with human beings. Telephoning, for example, to most organizations—department stores, government agencies, theaters, hotels, etc.—is an off-putting affair, in which programmed voices instruct the caller how to proceed. The arrangement is considered efficient, but it also provides encounters that are cold, unsatisfying, and often frustrating.

Corporate applications of electronic technology are forcing what remains of social connectedness into the crevices of American life. What this may mean for the future is beyond prediction, yet it cannot fail to be an influential factor, if and when the U.S. world position begins to weaken seriously. What can be expected of atomized and self-centered individuals when their assured levels of comfort and ease begin to contract?

Actually, the absence of social solidarity may already be

contributing to the weakening of the base of Numero Uno's global primacy. Growing inequality and a population devoid of cohesion are poor supports for the exercise of commanding world authority.

PATHOLOGICAL CONSUMERISM

Finally, a few words on a phenomenon of American life that invariably provokes the wonderment of most foreign visitors: the nonstop, round-the-clock promotion of consumerism. The U.S. informational system has been captured for marketing. The big sponsors, mostly consumer goods corporations, and their advertising agencies are the country's chief communicators. TV and radio are entirely financed by advertising, the press and magazines heavily so. Transmitting messages to buy goods, therefore, is the primary function of the world's most developed and capacious information technology.

Advertising expenditures in the United States, absolutely and on a per capita basis, are the highest in the world. No other population is subjected to such a concentrated barrage of salesmanship, which begins in infancy and continues until expiration. Some shopping malls are regarded as the equivalent of the Taj Mahal; tens of millions of Americans shop in them, sometimes traveling long distances to enjoy the experience.

On the face of it, consumerism would seem to be the ultimate soporific. Popular dissatisfaction seems to occur only when the shopping or the commercials are interrupted. In such an atmosphere, is there any reason to imagine that saturation

shopping could be a source of instability to the U.S. world position? Certainly not in any immediate or direct way! But just as
commercialization and commodification of life reduce the
human experience, obsessive consumerism dulls the person. A
country populated with shoppers is poorly prepared to assert,
much less back up, its worldwide dominance. This can only be
seen as positive, however one regards shopping. Shopping, not
soldiering, expresses the contemporary American outlook. This
may not be a heroic time, but it serves to lessen the options of
the governors of Numero Uno.

SOCIAL CONFLICT AND REGENERATION

If serious slippage does indeed occur in the United States' superpower role, the privileges accruing to this position soon will
begin to disappear. This is not a loss of intangible "prestige"; it
involves major material benefits to corporate shareholders,
some of which trickle down to the general population in jobs
and goods. Oil concessions in the Middle East, for example,
have not been ordained as U.S. corporate holdings in perpetuity.
Power secured them, and only power will retain them. Overseas markets for goods, financial entry to foreign capitals, and
airline landing rights are but a few of the potentially affected
activities if American power diminishes. With their curtailment,
domestic economic enterprise cannot fail to slacken and the
economy will most certainly slump.

The prospects on the international political scene are no
less grim for continued U.S. order giving. Ever more frequent

rebuffs may be expected as the ability of the United States to achieve consent through coercion diminishes. The United Nations, reduced to either irrelevancy or servility by U.S. treatment over five decades—the unwillingness to pay dues is but one of Washington's far from trivial slights—may regain an authoritative voice, one independent of Washington's influence. If in fact this occurs, many of the policies that the United States has pursued over the years will find support withdrawn, and unilateral actions to sustain American advantages in one or another part of the world may be too costly for a beleaguered superpower to exercise. As the *Foreign Affairs* editor puts it, we have "become a nation of cheap hawks."[14]

In the face of economic downturn and unaccustomed political resistance from abroad, what will be the reaction of the general public at home? Will its current indifference to anything happening outside U.S. borders change? And if it does, will the shift be toward empathy with others' concerns or the assumption of a combative xenophobia? Selective xenophobia has a long history in the United States.

Whatever the social direction that a reduced world role induces, one outcome seems assured: a sharp increase in social conflict between domestic haves and have-nots, a struggle over shares of diminishing resources.

This, surprisingly, could be a source of hope. The cocoon of indifference and self-satisfaction of the country's large middle class may begin to unspool. In a time of national adversity, especially when it is unevenly experienced, questioning, tension, and struggle cannot be contained—certainly not by routine political processes. In such a time of ferment, the creative energies of the population are bound to be stimulated. This does not mean that the energy automatically will flow in socially positive directions—but flow it will, and its direction will be determined partly by the public's perceived needs and partly by the strength of the participants in the social arena. In short, social conflict, embellished with class, racial, ethnic, and gender features, will reemerge. Undoubtedly, this will be disappointing to dominant social science, which long ago wrote off class struggle as obsolete. No matter.

What may be expected? Bland and vacuous politics, which have prevailed for so long, will be pushed off the nation's TV screens. Corporate informational control itself will be less effective when people's actual experiences contradict the media's messages more profoundly. Privatized spaces will be challenged and transformed into public sites of contestation. The dominant thinking and its assumptions, which have produced a crust of resistance to alternatives, may be on the verge of cracking.

As Numero Uno meets hard times, new ideas, new creativity, new social directions, and new institutional forms, though hardly certainties, may celebrate the next national historical turn. This is the hopeful scenario. The alternative, a repressive state run mainly in the interests of the well-off classes, is not precluded. It would be a national and international disaster.

NOTES

1. Fareed Zakaria, "Our Hollow Hegemony: The New American Consensus," *The*

New York Times Magazine, November l, 1998, 74.

2. Alan Cowell, "Plotting the Center of the New Europe," *The New York Times,* October 20, 1998, C-1.

3. Michael R. Sesit, "Currency Contenders," *Wall Street Journal,* September 28, 1998, R-18.

4. Ibid., quoting Professor Diana Kurz.

5. Erik Eckholm, "China: Europe Presses Trade Ties," *The New York Times,* October 30, 1998, A-8.

6. John Tagliabue, "Euro: Prenatal Force to Contend With," *The New York Times,* November 4, 1998, C-10.

7. Lester Thurow, *The Future of Capitalism* (New York: William Morrow, 1996), 195–196.

8. David Wessel and Bob Davis, "How Global Crisis Grew Despite Efforts of a Crack U.S. Team," *Wall Street Journal,* September 24, 1998, 1.

9. Richard W. Stevenson, "Europeans Challenge U.S. in Economic Crisis," *The New York Times,* October 7, 1998, 1.

10. Ibid.

11. Tim Weiner, "Big Cash Infusion Aims to Rebuild Anemic C.I.A.," *The New York Times,* October 22, 1998, A-3.

12. Steven A. Holmes, "Income Disparity Between Poorest and Richest Rises," *The New York Times,* June 20, 1996, 1.

13. Keith Bradsher, "Rich Control More U.S. Wealth, Study Says, as Debts Grow for Poor," *The New York Times,* June 22, 1996, 17.

14. Zakaria, "Our Hollow Hegemony."